P9-CQA-752

# Legalizing Marijuana,
## Second Edition

# POINT COUNTERPOINT

# Legalizing Marijuana,
## Second Edition

Paul Ruschmann, J.D.

SERIES EDITOR
Alan Marzilli, M.A., J.D.

CHELSEA HOUSE
PUBLISHERS
An imprint of Infobase Publishing

**Legalizing Marijuana, Second Edition**

Copyright © 2011 by Infobase Publishing

Chelsea House
An imprint of Infobase Publishing
132 West 31st Street
New York, NY 10001

**Library of Congress Cataloging-in-Publication Data**
Ruschmann, Paul.
  Legalizing marijuana / by Paul Ruschmann.—2nd ed.
  p. cm.—(Point/counterpoint)
  Includes bibliographical references and index.
  ISBN 978-1-60413-690-6 (hardcover)
  1. Marijuana—Law and legislation—United States—Juvenile literature. 2. Drug legalization—United States—Juvenile literature. I. Title. II. Series.
  KF3891.M2R87 2010
  345.73'0277—dc22
                            2009051404

Chelsea House books are available at special discounts when purchased in bulk quantities for businesses, associations, institutions, or sales promotions. Please call our Special Sales Department in New York at (212) 967-8800 or (800) 322-8755.

You can find Chelsea House on the World Wide Web at http://www.chelseahouse.com.

Text design by Keith Trego
Cover design by Alicia Post
Composition by EJB Publishing Services
Cover printed by Bang Printing, Brainerd, MN
Book printed and bound by Bang Printing, Brainerd, MN
Date printed: December 2010
Printed in the United States of America

10 9 8 7 6 5 4 3 2 1

**Alan Marzilli, M.A., J.D.**
**Birmingham, Alabama**

The POINT/COUNTERPOINT series offers the reader a greater under-standing of some of the most controversial issues in contemporary American society—issues such as capital punishment, immigration, gay rights, and gun control. We have looked for the most contem-porary issues and have included topics—such as the controversies surrounding "blogging"—that we could not have imagined when the series began.

In each volume, the author has selected an issue of particular importance and set out some of the key arguments on both sides of the issue. Why study both sides of the debate? Maybe you have yet to make up your mind on an issue, and the arguments presented in the book will help you to form an opinion. More likely, however, you will already have an opinion on many of the issues covered by the series. There is always the chance that you will change your opinion after reading the arguments for the other side. But even if you are firmly committed to an issue—for example, school prayer or animal rights—reading both sides of the argument will help you to become a more effective advo-cate for your cause. By gaining an understanding of opposing argu-ments, you can develop answers to those arguments.

Perhaps more importantly, listening to the other side sometimes helps you see your opponent's arguments in a more human way. For example, Sister Helen Prejean, one of the nation's most visible oppo-nents of capital punishment, has been deeply affected by her interac-tions with the families of murder victims. By seeing the families' grief and pain, she understands much better why people support the death penalty, and she is able to carry out her advocacy with a greater sensi-tivity to the needs and beliefs of death penalty supporters.

The books in the series include numerous features that help the reader to gain a greater understanding of the issues. Real-life examples illustrate the human side of the issues. Each chapter also includes excerpts from relevant laws, court cases, and other material, which provide a better foundation for understanding the arguments. The volumes contain citations to relevant sources of law and information, and an appendix guides the reader through the basics of legal research, both on the Internet and in the library. Today, through free Web sites, it is easy to access legal documents, and these books might give you ideas for your own research.

Studying the issues covered by the POINT/COUNTERPOINT series is more than an academic activity. The issues described in the books affect all of us as citizens. They are the issues that today's leaders debate and tomorrow's leaders will decide. While all of the issues covered in the POINT/COUNTERPOINT series are controversial today, and will remain so for the foreseeable future, it is entirely possible that the reader might one day play a central role in resolving the debate. Today it might seem that some debates—such as capital punishment and abortion—will never be resolved.

However, our nation's history is full of debates that seemed as though they never would be resolved, and many of the issues are now well settled—at least on the surface. In the nineteenth century, abolitionists met with widespread resistance to their efforts to end slavery. Ultimately, the controversy threatened the union, leading to the Civil War between the northern and southern states. Today, while a public debate over the merits of slavery would be unthinkable, racism persists in many aspects of society.

Similarly, today nobody questions women's right to vote. Yet at the beginning of the twentieth century, suffragists fought public battles for women's voting rights, and it was not until the passage of the Nineteenth Amendment in 1920 that the legal right of women to vote was established nationwide.

What makes an issue controversial? Often, controversies arise when most people agree that there is a problem but disagree about the best way to solve it. There is little argument that poverty is a major problem in the United States, especially in inner cities and rural areas. Yet, people disagree vehemently about the best way to address the problem. To some, the answer is social programs, such as welfare, food stamps, and public housing. However, many argue that such subsidies encourage dependence on government benefits while unfairly penalizing those who work and pay taxes, and that the real solution is to require people to support themselves.

American society is in a constant state of change, and sometimes modern practices clash with what many consider to be "traditional values," which are often rooted in conservative political views or religious beliefs. Many blame high crime rates, and problems such as poverty, illiteracy, and drug use on the breakdown of the traditional family structure of a married mother and father raising their children. Since the "sexual revolution" of the 1960s and 1970s, sparked in part by the widespread availability of the birth control pill, marriage rates have declined, and the number of children born outside of marriage has increased. The sexual revolution led to controversies over birth control, sex education, and other issues, most prominently abortion. Similarly, the gay rights movement has been challenged as a threat to traditional values. While many gay men and lesbians want to have the same right to marry and raise families as heterosexuals, many politicians and others have challenged gay marriage and adoption as a threat to American society.

Sometimes, new technology raises issues that we have never faced before, and society disagrees about the best solution. Are people free to swap music online, or does this violate the copyright laws that protect songwriters and musicians' ownership of the music that they create? Should scientists use "genetic engineering" to create new crops that are resistant to disease and pests and produce more food, or is it too risky to use a laboratory to create plants that nature never intended? Modern medicine has continued to increase the average lifespan—which is now 77 years, up from under 50 years at the beginning of the twentieth century—but many people are now choosing to die in comfort rather than living with painful ailments in their later years. For doctors, this presents an ethical dilemma: should they allow their patients to die? Should they assist patients in ending their own lives painlessly?

Perhaps the most controversial issues are those that implicate a Constitutional right. The Bill of Rights—the first 10 Amendments to the U.S. Constitution—spells out some of the most fundamental rights that distinguish our democracy from other nations with fewer freedoms. However, the sparsely worded document is open to interpretation, with each side saying that the Constitution is on their side. The Bill of Rights was meant to protect individual liberties; however, the needs of some individuals clash with society's needs. Thus, the Constitution often serves as a battleground between individuals and government officials seeking to protect society in some way. The First Amendment's guarantee of "freedom of speech" leads to some very difficult questions. Some forms of expression—such as burning an American flag—lead to public outrage, but are protected by the First Amendment. Other types of expression that most people find objectionable—such as child pornography—are not protected by the Constitution. The question is not only where to draw the line, but whether drawing lines around constitutional rights threatens our liberty.

The Bill of Rights raises many other questions about individual rights and societal "good." Is a prayer before a high school football game an "establishment of religion" prohibited by the First Amendment? Does the Second Amendment's promise of "the right to bear arms" include concealed handguns? Does stopping and frisking someone standing on a known drug corner constitute "unreasonable search and seizure" in violation of the Fourth Amendment? Although the U.S. Supreme Court has the ultimate authority in interpreting the U.S. Constitution, its answers do not always satisfy the public. When a group of nine people—sometimes by a five-to-four vote—makes a decision that affects hundreds of millions of others, public outcry can be expected. For example, the Supreme Court's 1973 ruling in *Roe v. Wade* that abortion is protected by the Constitution did little to quell the debate over abortion.

Whatever the root of the controversy, the books in the POINT/ COUNTERPOINT series seek to explain to the reader the origins of the debate, the current state of the law, and the arguments on either side of the debate. Our hope in creating this series is that readers will be better informed about the issues facing not only our politicians, but all of our nation's citizens, and become more actively involved in resolving these debates, as voters, concerned citizens, journalists, or maybe even elected officials.

Since the first edition of *Legalizing Marijuana* was published, there have been a number of legal developments. Several state legislatures have reconsidered their overall policies toward possession of marijuana for personal use, and state "medical marijuana" laws have led to the proliferation of well-organized dispensaries offering patients a variety of choices of marijuana. The Obama administration announced that it would not raid these clinics in states that have legalized medical marijuana. While medical marijuana remains controversial, a significant percentage of Americans believe that even recreational use should be allowed. With jails and prisons facing overcrowding, many question whether the government should use its resources to fight other types of crime. Further, they argue, the illegality of marijuana allows violent drug gangs to control distribution, violence that would be diminished if legitimate businesses were allowed to produce and sell marijuana. The federal government, however, has maintained its position that non-medical use of marijuana is a crime, and many experts point to its harmful effects, including the often-debated idea that it is a "gateway" to drugs such as heroin. This volume examines these and other controversies that continue to capture the attention of state and federal lawmakers.

# Marijuana and Prohibition

When its 2009 session began, the California Legislature's top priority was dealing with a huge budget deficit. Tom Ammiano, a lawmaker from San Francisco, offered an unusual proposal[1] aimed at raising revenue: legalizing and taxing marijuana in the state. Governor Arnold Schwarzenegger said the time had come to debate legalization, and a statewide poll found 56 percent of Californians were in favor of it.

Even though Ammiano's bill failed to get out of committee, it gained nationwide media coverage. Many Americans believe that a new chapter has begun in the debate over our nation's marijuana policy: Public officials are giving serious thought to ending prohibition. The current debate is a far cry from a generation ago, when marijuana was a symbol of protest and the drug divided Americans along cultural and generational lines. There are, however, still deep and emotional differences of opinion about marijuana.

## What is Marijuana and Who Uses It?

Marijuana is one of many mood-altering substances used by humans. The law classifies the drug as a hallucinogen—a substance that distorts the user's perception of reality—and places it in the same class as LSD. Marijuana comes from the flowers and leaves of the cannabis plant, which grows as a weed in much of the world. The cannabis plant, raised for years to make linen and rope, is a source of birdseed and oil used in paints.

Among the hundreds of chemicals in marijuana, the principal active ingredient is 1-delta-9-trans tetrahydrocannabinol, commonly known as THC. The THC content of marijuana varies, depending on the strain of plant it comes from and how much of it is taken from high-THC parts of the plant. The National Institute on Drug Abuse (NIDA) describes marijuana's effect on the user:

> When marijuana is smoked, its effects begin immediately after the drug enters the brain and last from 1 to 3 hours. . . . Within a few minutes after inhaling marijuana smoke, an individual's heart begins beating more rapidly, the bronchial passages relax and become enlarged, and blood vessels in the eyes expand, making the eyes look red. The heart rate, normally 70 to 80 beats per minute, may increase by 20 to 50 beats per minute or, in some cases, even double. . . .
>
> As THC enters the brain, it causes a user to feel euphoric—or "high"—by acting in the brain's reward system, areas of the brain that respond to stimuli such as food and drink. . . .
>
> A marijuana user may experience pleasant sensations, colors and sounds may seem more intense, and time appears to pass very slowly. . . . The euphoria passes after awhile, and then the user may feel sleepy or depressed. Occasionally, marijuana use produces anxiety, fear, distrust, or panic.[2]

The intensity of a marijuana high depends on the potency of the marijuana, whether it is smoked or eaten, the user's personality and experience, and the surroundings in which it is used.

In the United States, marijuana is the most commonly used illegal drug. According to recent surveys, about 100 million Americans have used it at least once in their lives, and an estimated 14.6 million, or 6.2 percent, are "current users," meaning they have used it within the past year. Marijuana is most popular with teenagers and young adults. The 2008 Monitoring the Future study of drug use by young people found that 10.9 percent of eighth-graders, 23.9 percent of tenth-graders, and 32.4 percent of twelfth-graders had used marijuana during the previous year. Marijuana use peaks during the late teenage years, and declines steadily afterward, with all but a few giving it up by age 30. Although most marijuana users are "experimenters" who try it a few times, a small percentage become heavy users, and run the risk of having trouble at school or work or developing serious health problems.

## A Short History of Marijuana

Thousands of years ago, marijuana was used in China and India for medicinal purposes and in religious ceremonies. From Asia, marijuana spread to ancient Egypt and Greece, to tribes living in Africa, and later, to Europe and the Americas. The Jamestown settlers brought the cannabis plant to Virginia, where they raised it to produce hemp, which was used to produce rope for ships. Hemp was an important crop in America until after the Civil War. It made a brief comeback during World War II: After the Japanese seized the Pacific hemp crop, American farmers grew the plant to make rope for Navy ships.

According to the editors of *Consumer Reports*:

In short, marijuana was readily available in the United States through much of the nineteenth and early twentieth centuries, its effects were known, and it was occasionally used for recreational purposes. But use was at best limited, local, and temporary. Not until after 1920 did marijuana come into general use—and not until the 1960s did it become a popular drug.[3]

Recreational marijuana use became associated with immigrants and members of racial minorities, and this clash of cultures played a significant role in marijuana becoming illegal.

## America Prohibits Marijuana

A century ago, marijuana, opium, and even cocaine and heroin were legal in America and used mostly to relieve medical conditions. Some versions were sold over the counter, as aspirin and cough medicine are today. Several factors led to the passage of laws restricting the availability of these drugs: growing awareness of their addictive nature; a desire by the medical profession to control their distribution; and, significantly, many Americans' opposition, on moral grounds, to taking drugs for pleasure. Since colonial times, activities such as gambling, sex outside marriage, and even card playing were seen as vices. Substance abuse was considered particularly offensive:

> One 18th century pamphleteer advised against the use of any drink "which is liable to steal away a man's senses and render him foolish, irascible, uncontrollable and dangerous." Similarly, one 19th century observer attributed delirium tremens, perverted sexuality, impotency, insanity and cancer to the smoking and chewing of tobacco.[4]

As the twentieth century began, opposition to recreational drug use, much of which was encouraged by religious leaders, reached the point that some state lawmakers tried to prohibit the use of alcohol and tobacco as well as opium products.

In 1914, Congress passed the Harrison Narcotics Tax Act (Harrison Act).[5] According to the editors of *Consumer Reports*:

# Decline in teen pot use stalls

The use of marijuana has leveled off after nearly a decade of steady decline.

**Marijuana use,** in the 12 months prior to the survey

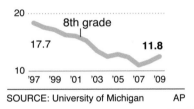

SOURCE: University of Michigan          AP

This graphic shows marijuana use by eighth and twelfth graders in the United States since 1997. Although marijuana use had been trending downward for a decade, recent years have shown an increase in usage.

"Far from appearing to be a prohibition law, the Harrison Narcotic Act on its face was merely a law for the orderly marketing of opium, morphine, heroin, and other drugs—in small quantities over the counter, and in larger quantities on a physician's prescription."[6] After the act took effect, however, federal authorities interpreted that language to mean that a doctor could not prescribe opiates to an addict to maintain his addiction. In two 1919 cases, *United States v. Doremus* and *Webb v. United States*, the Supreme Court agreed with the government.

Although the Harrison Act did not apply to marijuana, a growing number of states and cities outlawed the drug, often in response to sensational newspaper stories that exaggerated the prevalence of marijuana use and its harmful effects. At the

## FROM THE BENCH

### *United States v. Doremus*, 249 U.S. 86 (1919) and *Webb v. United States*, 249 U.S. 96 (1919)

In 1914, Congress passed the Harrison Narcotic Drug Act. At the time, the U.S. Supreme Court took a narrow view of Congress's power to regulate interstate commerce. As a result, lawmakers relied on Article 1, Section 8 of the U.S. Constitution, which authorizes Congress to levy and collect taxes, as authority for the act.

Section 1 of the act required those who distributed opium, coca leaves, or any derivative of those substances to register with the government and pay a $1-per-year tax. Section 2 provided that narcotics could be distributed only to individuals who presented a government-approved order form, and required those who distributed narcotics to keep the order forms for two years afterward.

The act contained language stating that it did not apply "(a) To the dispensing or distribution of any of the aforesaid drugs to a patient by a physician . . . in the course of his professional practice only" and "(b) To the sale, dispensing, or distribution of any of the aforesaid drugs by a dealer to a consumer under and in pursuance of a written prescription" only to the extent of requiring them to keep a record of prescriptions written and filled.

Some historians believe that Congress passed the Harrison Act to ensure the orderly marketing of narcotics, not to prohibit their use. Nevertheless, the government treated the act as a prohibition law, taking the position that maintaining an addict's narcotics habit was not a legitimate part of a doctor's "professional practice."

Two constitutional challenges to the government's interpretation of the Harrison Act eventually reached the Supreme Court. *United States v. Doremus* involved a doctor who dispensed heroin to an addict "for the purpose of gratifying his appetite for the drug as an habitual user." Dr. Doremus argued that the Harrison Act was unconstitutional because it was not a tax measure but really an attempt to regulate narcotics, which fell within the states' power to pass laws to promote public welfare.

same time, Harry Anslinger, the head of the federal Bureau of Narcotics, waged a campaign to eliminate marijuana use. That campaign, which relied on exaggeration and fear, was successful: Nearly every state outlawed the recreational use of marijuana,

The second case, *Webb v. United States*, involved the prosecution of a Dr. Webb and Goldbaum, a drugstore owner. Dr. Webb had a number of patients who were addicted to morphine. Instead of attempting to cure their addiction to the drug, he gave them prescriptions for enough morphine to keep them comfortable. Goldbaum filled thousands of those prescriptions. Even though both Webb and Goldbaum complied with the Harrison Act's paperwork requirements and paid the required taxes, federal officials nonetheless charged them with violating the act. Both men were convicted.

In both cases, the Supreme Court ruled in favor of the government by a 5-to-4 vote. Justice William Day wrote the majority opinions. In *Doremus*, Day held that the Harrison Act was a legitimate exercise of Congress's power to tax. So long as a law had "some reasonable relation" to the taxing power, it would be upheld, even though lawmakers might have had some other motive for passing it and the businesses taxed were also subject to the states' police powers. In the case of narcotics, Day reasoned, Congress reasonably could have concluded that regulating and taxing them would keep the traffic aboveboard and open to inspection, and would make it harder for unauthorized persons to get narcotics and sell them on the black market. He added that the act might also stop patients from re-selling some of the drugs prescribed to them. In *Webb*, Day held that the Harrison Act's requirement, that a person produce an order blank to buy narcotics, was constitutional. He also concluded that the language in the act that referred to "his professional practice only" barred a doctor from prescribing a narcotic to keep an maintain a patient's addiction rather than help him end it.

Chief Justice Edward White wrote a brief dissent in *Doremus* in which he argued that the Harrison Act was "a mere attempt by Congress to exert a power not delegated, that is, the reserved police power of the states." He did not write a dissenting opinion in *Webb*.

Marijuana was not regulated under federal law until Congress passed the Marijuana Tax Act of 1937. The drug was not fully prohibited under federal law until Congress passed the Controlled Substances Act in 1970.

and usually imposed penalties as harsh as those for heroin or cocaine. Anslinger also campaigned for federal legislation. He succeeded in 1937, when Congress passed the Marijuana Tax Act.[7] Like the Harrison Act, this was a tax measure rather than out-and-out prohibition, but it made the drug all but impossible to obtain.

In those days, marijuana users were viewed as addicts and part of the "criminal element," an assumption that made it easier to assume that the drug caused crime and violence. In recommending that the Marijuana Tax Act be passed, the House Ways and Means Committee reported: "Under the influence of this drug the will is destroyed and all power of directing and controlling thought is lost. Inhibitions are released. As a result of these effects, it appeared from testimony produced at the hearings that many violent crimes have been and are being committed by persons under the influence of this drug."[8]

In the years that followed, lawmakers believed that severe penalties for selling and using drugs would deter drug use— that is, persuade would-be users not to try them. When drug use persisted, Congress and the states passed even tougher laws. The Boggs Act of 1951 provided for mandatory minimum sentences for drug offenses, including marijuana. Five years later, Congress passed the even tougher Narcotic Control Act. Policymakers also believed that marijuana inevitably led to the use of "harder," or more dangerous, drugs. A senator who supported that legislation said: "Marijuana is a drug which starts most addicts in the use of drugs. . . . Evidently, its use leads to the heroin habit and then to the final destruction of the persons addicted."[9] His comment was typical of policymakers' perception of marijuana as a "gateway" drug. The law also incorrectly defined marijuana as a narcotic—a drug that produces sleep or stupor—and put it in the same class as heroin and cocaine. Lawmakers treated marijuana as a serious menace even though studies, going back to the British Government's Indian Hemp Drugs Commission in 1894, found that marijuana posed less of a risk of dependence than many opponents claimed it did.

## "Culture Wars" and Second Thoughts

When the 1960s began, marijuana use was limited to the lower social and economic classes, along with jazz musicians, artists, and writers. Then it suddenly spread to mainstream America, beginning with college students. The popularity of marijuana coincided with the Vietnam War and the sexual revolution, both of which divided the generations. Some young people used marijuana as a protest against their elders. Once again, the drug became associated with undesirables: this time, "hippies," a sub-group of young people who were characterized by an unkempt appearance, lack of a work ethic, left-wing political views, and a tendency to use illegal drugs.

When marijuana became popular, harsh laws were still on the books in many states. Prosecutors allowed most offenders to plead guilty to a less-serious offense and avoid a mandatory sentence. A few people, however, whose behavior society found offensive, were punished to the full extent of the law. One such individual was musician John Sinclair, who also founded the radical White Panther Party. Sinclair's radical politics attracted the attention of the police, who caught him in a marijuana "sting" operation. He was convicted of giving two marijuana cigarettes to undercover police officers and sentenced to 10 years in prison under Michigan's tough narcotics law. Sinclair's case attracted worldwide attention. Ultimately, in *People v. Sinclair* (1972), the Supreme Court of Michigan unanimously threw out his conviction.

Although most Americans thought using marijuana was wrong, many considered the penalties for using it out of proportion to the offense. Congress addressed the issue in 1970, as part of a larger effort to replace a patchwork of drug laws with the Comprehensive Drug Abuse Prevention and Control Act.[10] Title II of the act, the Controlled Substances Act (CSA), made possession and use of small amounts of marijuana a less-serious offense, and also allowed judges to drop the charges if the accused lived up to the terms of probation. On the other hand, the CSA placed marijuana in Schedule I of controlled substances, which meant that it had a high potential for abuse and no legitimate use in medicine.

Congress also created a commission to study marijuana policy, headed by former governor Raymond Shafer of Pennsylvania.

## THE LETTER OF THE LAW

## Federal Marijuana Penalties

Most marijuana arrests are made under state laws. Federal laws, however, have strong symbolic value, and in the future, they might become a barrier to liberalizing state and local marijuana laws.

In 1970, Congress passed the Controlled Substances Act (CSA), which reduced the penalties for possessing or giving away small amounts of marijuana, but continued to treat it as a crime. During the 1970s, Congress rejected the Shafer Commission's recommendations that penalties for possession and use be abolished. When the "war on drugs" began in the 1980s, lawmakers amended the CSA to provide for more severe penalties, especially for those involved with large amounts of marijuana.

On its Web site*, the National Organization for the Reform of Marijuana Laws (NORML) has summarized federal marijuana penalties.

### Penalties for simple possession of marijuana:

First offense: Misdemeanor, punishable a fine of up to $1,000 and up to one year in jail. A provision of the CSA gives the government the option of imposing a civil penalty of up to $10,000 on a first offender charged with possession of a "personal use" amount of a drug.

Second offense: Misdemeanor, punishable by a fine of to $2,500 and up to two years in prison (mandatory minimum of 15 days).

Third or subsequent offense: Either a misdemeanor or a felony, punishable by a fine of up to $5,000 and up to three years in prison (mandatory minimum of 90 days).

In 1972, the commission released its report, *Marijuana: A Signal of Misunderstanding.* The Shafer Commission found:

> Marijuana's relative potential for harm to the vast majority of individual users and its actual impact on society does not justify a social policy designed to seek out and firmly punish those who use it. This judgment is

*(continues on page 24)*

### Penalties for selling or growing marijuana:

Giving a small amount of marijuana to a person 21 or older is treated the same as simple possession.

Selling or growing of less than 50 kilograms (one kilogram equals 2.2 pounds) is a felony, punishable by a fine of up to $250,000 and up to five years in prison.

Selling or growing more than 50 kilograms is also a felony. The maximum penalties depend on the amount involved. If the amount is between 50 and 100 kilograms, the maximum penalty is 20 years in prison and a $1 million fine. If the amount is between 100 and 1,000 kilograms, the maximum penalty is 40 years in prison and a $2 million fine. If the quantity is greater than 1,000 kilograms, the maximum penalty is life in prison and a $4 million fine.

A person who distributes marijuana to a person younger than 21, or who distributes it in a "drug-free zone" such as a school, a college, public housing, a video arcade, a youth center, or a public pool, may be sentenced to double the maximum penalties.

### Death penalty for drug "kingpins":

An organizer or leader of a "continuing criminal enterprise" that either handles 60,000 kilograms or more of a mixture containing marijuana or grosses more than $20 million within any 12-month period may be sentenced to death.

* http://www.norml.org/index.cfm?wtm_view=&Group_ID=4575.

## FROM THE BENCH

### *People v. Sinclair*, 387 Mich. 91, 194 N.W.2d 878 (1972)

*People v. Sinclair* is one of the most famous marijuana cases in American history. Even by the standards of the 1960s, the criminal justice system treated Sinclair harshly for what many present-day Americans consider a minor offense. He was given a 10-year prison sentence for giving two marijuana cigarettes to undercover police officers.

In addition to whether punishment fit the crime, the Sinclair case raised other issues, including whether the authorities targeted Sinclair for his political views—he founded the radical White Panther Party—and whether investigative tactics used by the police were lawful. Sinclair appealed his conviction, and his appeal eventually reached the Supreme Court of Michigan. Even though the justices unanimously agreed that Sinclair should not have been sentenced to a long prison term, they reached that conclusion for varying reasons.

Justice John Swainson, who wrote the majority opinion, concluded that Michigan denied Sinclair equal protection of the law by unreasonably placing marijuana in the same category as "hard" drugs:

> [T]he issue is whether marijuana may be constitutionally classified as a narcotic drug if, in fact, it is not a narcotic. . . .
>
> Comparison of the effects of marijuana use on both the individual and society with the effects of other drug use demonstrates not only that there is no rational basis for classifying marijuana with the "hard narcotics," but, also, that there is not even a rational basis for treating marijuana as a more dangerous drug than alcohol. . . .
>
> Marijuana is a mild hallucinogen, which in view of its lack of any other harmful effects, leads us to conclude that there is no rational basis for penalizing it more severely than the other hallucinogens. . . .
>
> Virtually every major commission which has studied the effects of marijuana use agrees that it is improperly classified with the "hard" narcotics. . . .
>
> We can no longer allow the residuals of that early misinformation to continue choking off a rational evaluation of marijuana dangers. That a large and increasing number of Americans recognize the truth about marijuana's relative harmlessness can scarcely be doubted.

Swainson also concluded that the police had violated Sinclair's constitutional rights by entrapping him:

The two marijuana cigarettes obtained purely as a result of illegal police conduct were the sole basis of defendant's conviction. . . . If the conviction stands, the police can ignore with impunity the doctrine of entrapment in narcotic cases. Citizens could be enticed and entrapped to give marijuana to police undercover agents, using methods condemned by the courts of this State and our sister states. . . .

Defendant did not volunteer the two cigarettes to the undercover agents; he only gave the cigarettes to them after repeated requests by the officers, who had deceived him over a lengthy period of time.

Justice G. Mennen Williams agreed with the majority that Michigan's narcotics law had denied Sinclair equal protection of the law because it classified marijuana as a "hard drug," even though other hallucinogenic drugs such as LSD, peyote, and mescaline were grouped together and the penalties for using those drugs were less severe. He also said: "This is an opinion concerning a problem whose time has come. The name in the entitling is happenstance as the defendant could have been any mother's son or daughter."

Justice Thomas G. Kavanagh agreed with the majority that the police had illegally entrapped Sinclair, but also maintained that they had violated his constitutional right to privacy:

I find that our statute violates the Federal and State constitutions in that it is an impermissible intrusion on the fundamental rights to liberty and the pursuit of happiness, and is an unwarranted interference with the right to possess and use private property.

As I understand our constitutional concept of government, an individual is free to do whatever he pleases, so long as he does not interfere with the rights of his neighbor or of society. . . .

Whatever the validity of the concept that traffic in marijuana is freighted with a proper public interest, it is extending the concept entirely too far to sanction proscription of possession and private use of marijuana.

Finally, Justice Thomas Brennan argued that Sinclair's 10-year sentence violated the Constitution's ban on cruel and unusual punishment. He pointed out that since 1964, a total of 1,663 defendants were charged with possession of marijuana. Of those defendants, 467 were sent to prison, 46 received sentences of five years or longer, and only five were sentenced to more than five years for possession of any amount or any kind of narcotic.

*(continued from page 21)*

based on prevalent use patterns, on behavior exhibited by the vast majority of users and on our interpretations of existing medical and scientific data.[11]

The Shafer Commission called for the repeal of laws against private possession and use, but federal and state lawmakers rejected the idea. Only one state—Alaska—actually did so, and that was the result of a court decision, not legislation. In *State v. Ravin* (1975), that state's highest court concluded that the constitutional right to privacy extended to adults using the drug at home. The first state to pass legislation decriminalizing the drug was Oregon, which, in 1973, downgraded the possession of less than an ounce of marijuana to a "civil violation" punishable by a $100 fine. Today, 11 states have eliminated jail as a punishment for the possession of small amounts of the drug. Some of these states classify the offense as civil in nature, while others treat it as a very low-level misdemeanor. The remaining states, however, treat possession and use, even of small amounts, as a misdemeanor that carries the possibility of jail time and a criminal record.

During the 1980s, concern over drug use, crack cocaine in particular, led the nation to declare a "war on drugs." Penalties became more severe, especially for repeat offenders and those dealing in large quantities; mandatory penalties reappeared; and the federal government spent large sums of money on law enforcement. States took a harder line as well. The result was a sharp increase in the number of people arrested and put behind bars for drug offenses. At the same time, the government and the media launched a massive campaign to discourage Americans, especially young people, from using drugs. First Lady Nancy Reagan urged Americans to "just say no" to drugs; and commercials showing a frying egg warned, "This is your brain on drugs." The war on drugs continues to this day. The official policy of the U.S. government is a "drug-free America," and the recreational use of marijuana is against the law everywhere in the country.

## The Return of Medical Marijuana

Marijuana has been used by doctors for centuries—one of history's most famous marijuana patients was Queen Victoria of Great Britain—and the drug was used to treat many of the same medical conditions for which some present-day doctors recommend marijuana. During the twentieth century, the drug fell out of favor because effective pain relievers had come on the market and the medical profession had become more sophisticated. Nevertheless, many state laws permitted medical marijuana, and the drug was recognized by the medical profession as recently as 1942.

After the CSA banned medical marijuana in 1970, some members of the health care community campaigned for its re-legalization. Their efforts paid off in 1996, when California voters approved Proposition 215, the Compassionate Use Act. The purpose of that law was "[t]o ensure that seriously ill Californians have the right to obtain and use marijuana for medical purposes where that medical use is deemed appropriate and has been recommended by a physician who has determined that the person's health would benefit from the use of marijuana."[12] As of January 2010, 14 states had enacted some form of medical-marijuana law.

State medical-marijuana laws protect patients, and those who supply them with marijuana, from prosecution by state authorities. Federal authorities, however, can arrest and prosecute them under the CSA, regardless of what state law provides. The federal government has opposed medical-marijuana laws from the start. Soon after California legalized medical marijuana in 1996, the federal government responded by strictly enforcing the CSA. In the years that followed, federal agents raided more than 100 medical marijuana growers and dispensaries; and U.S. attorneys brought charges under the CSA against a number of individuals who supplied the drug to patients. More than a dozen people were sent to prison on federal drug charges.

In *United States v. Oakland Cannabis Buyers' Cooperative* (2001), the U.S. Supreme Court rejected the argument that suppliers of marijuana had a "medical necessity" defense against being prosecuted under the CSA. The justices said:

> Under any conception of a legal necessity, one principle is clear: The [medical necessity] defense cannot succeed when the legislature itself has made a "determination of values." In the case of the Controlled Substances Act, the statute reflects a determination that marijuana has no medical benefits worthy of an exception.[13]

Four years later, in *Gonzalez v. Raich* (2005), the Court turned down another challenge to the CSA, ruling that the law applied even to the noncommercial use of medical marijuana. Since President Barack Obama took office in January 2009, the federal government has retreated somewhat from its hard-line stance toward medical marijuana. In early 2009, Attorney General Eric Holder indicated that federal agents would deemphasize enforcement action against providers and users in states where medical marijuana was legal.

## Summary

People have used marijuana for thousands of years, especially for religious and medical reasons. American policymakers, however, outlawed the drug because they assumed that it caused violent crime and addiction. Those laws called for heavy punishment for sellers and users. During the 1960s, young people from middle-class families started to use the drug. The result was a re-examination of marijuana policy and the passage of laws that carry lighter penalties for possessing or using small amounts. Some Americans argue that laws prohibiting marijuana should be relaxed, or even done away with. A number of states have authorized the use of marijuana for medical purposes. Federal law, however, forbids marijuana use entirely, and all states continue to prohibit it for recreational purposes.

# Government Should Protect People from Marijuana

Deciding whether to outlaw certain behavior, such as smoking marijuana, is not an exact science. Instead, it is largely a value judgment. In the words of the Shafer Commission: "The issue is really to determine when the undesirable effect upon others is likely enough or direct enough for society to take cognizance of it and to deal with it. Coupled with this is the further question of whether the nature of the behavior and its possible effect is such that society should employ coercive measures."[1] The principal reason why marijuana is illegal is that policymakers consider it dangerous. Supporters of marijuana prohibition can point to a considerable amount of evidence that the drug is harmful, not only to the user but to society as a whole.

## Marijuana use can lead to dependence.

A report by the Office of National Drug Control Policy (ONDCP) explains: "According to the 2002 National Survey on Drug Use and

Health, 4.3 million Americans were classified with dependence on or abuse of marijuana. That figure represents 1.8 percent of the total U.S. population and 60.3 percent of those classified as individuals who abuse or are dependent on illicit drugs."[2] Frequent users run a high risk of becoming dependent. Roger Roffman, a professor at the University of Washington, notes that marijuana dependence occurs in nine percent of Americans who have ever used the drug, but ranges between 33 percent and 50 percent among those who use it daily or almost daily.

A growing number of users need treatment to break their dependence. In 2003, one-fifth of the more than 900,000 adults who went into treatment for illegal drug abuse named marijuana as their primary drug of abuse. Roffman notes that those who sought help averaged 10 years of daily or near-daily use and had unsuccessfully tried to quit more than six times. Dependence among young people is a particular concern. According to the Drug Enforcement Administration (DEA), the number of teenagers in treatment who reported marijuana as the primary substance of abuse increased sharply between 1993 and 2003; and in 2003, more people ages 12 to 17 entered treatment in marijuana dependency than for alcohol. Scott Burns, an official at the ONDCP, points out that 60 percent of teenagers who are in treatment for drugs have a primary marijuana diagnosis—more than for alcohol and all illegal drugs combined.

## Marijuana is linked to crime.

People with criminal records are more likely to have a history of marijuana use than law-abiding citizens.

In 2002, the National Institute of Justice's Arrestee Drug Abuse Monitoring (ADAM) Program, which collects data on the number of adult arrestees testing positive for various drugs, found that, on average, 41 percent of adult male arrestees and 27 percent of adult female arrestees tested positive for marijuana. On average, 57 percent of juvenile male and 32 percent of juvenile female arrestees tested positive for marijuana.[3]

## What Is Dependence?

Studies show that many thousands of marijuana users are at risk of developing a dependence on the drug. What does "dependence" mean, and how do we know whether someone is dependent? In *The Diagnostic and Statistical Manual of Mental Disorders, Fourth Edition*, the American Psychiatric Association has identified the following criteria for dependence on marijuana or some other drug:

Substance dependence is a maladaptive pattern of substance use, leading to clinically significant impairment or distress, as manifested by three (or more) of the following, occurring at any time in the same 12-month period:

1. Tolerance, as defined by either of the following:

    a. A need for markedly increased amounts of the substance to achieve intoxication or desired effect;

    b. Markedly diminished effect with continued use of the same amount of the substance.

2. Withdrawal, as manifested by either of the following:

    a. The characteristic withdrawal syndrome for the substance;

    b. The same (or a closely related) substance is taken to relieve or avoid withdrawal symptoms.

3. The substance is often taken in larger amounts or over a longer period than was intended;

4. There is a persistent desire or unsuccessful efforts to cut down or control substance use;

5. A great deal of time is spent on activities necessary to obtain the substance, use the substance, or recover from its effects;

6. Important social, occupational, or recreational activities are given up or reduced because of substance use;

7. The substance use is continued despite knowledge of having a persistent or recurrent physical or psychological problem that is likely to have been caused or exacerbated by the substance.

Source: American Psychiatric Association, *Diagnostic and Statistical Manual of Mental Disorders, Fourth Edition*. Arlington, Va.: American Psychiatric Publishing, 2000.

A follow-up study found that the percentage of arrestees who tested positive for the drug had remained "remarkably stable" since data collection began in 2000. More generally, marijuana has been linked to a range of antisocial behavior on the part of young people. A study cited by the DEA found that teenagers who use the drug once a week were more likely to run away from home, steal, engage in violence, and have suicidal thoughts.

Americans' use of marijuana—by one estimate, $10 billion a year is spent on the drug—helps fund violent drug cartels. In Mexico, these cartels are involved in a vicious conflict with the authorities and with one another. That conflict is responsible for more than 6,000 killings per year in Mexico, and the violence spread to cities in this country. Marijuana users also support homegrown drug gangs in our nation's cities. Former ONDCP Director John Walters commented on one such gang operating in Washington, D.C.:

> [T]he K Street Crew was a vicious group of marijuana dealers whose decade-long reign of terror was brought to an end only this year after a massive prosecution effort by Michael Volkov, chief gang prosecutor for the U.S. attorney's office. The K Street Crew is credited with at least 17 murders, including systematic killings of potential witnesses. . . .
>
> Says prosecutor Volkov: "The experience in D.C. shows that marijuana dealers are no less violent than cocaine and heroin traffickers. They have just as much money to lose, just as much turf to lose, and just as many reasons to kill as any drug trafficker."[4]

## Marijuana is a "gateway" to other drugs.

Marijuana users are more likely than nonusers to use more dangerous substances. The ONDCP's Scott Burns points out that people who used marijuana are eight times more likely to have used cocaine, 15 times more likely to have used heroin, and five times more likely to develop a need for treatment of abuse or dependence on *any* drug. Studies also show that heavy marijuana users, and those who started using the drug at an early age, are at higher risk of using "harder" drugs.

Using marijuana exposes the user to a culture that encourages the use of harder drugs as well. The Shafer Commission found:

> The more one smokes marijuana, the more involved his interpersonal relationships are likely to become with his peers who share the experience with him. As he spends more time with this group, he begins to sever his contacts with conventional individuals and conventional routines. He may eventually view himself as a drug user and be willing to experiment with other drugs which are approved by his peer group.[5]

Marijuana also exposes the user to "polydrug" use—the use of two or more substances at the same time—which is a more serious health menace than using marijuana alone. Gangs that sell marijuana often traffic in heroin and cocaine as well. Also, a variety of drugs in addition to marijuana are commonly available at parties, clubs, and concerts. Marijuana users may even consume other drugs without knowing it. There have been reports that some marijuana has been laced with other substances, including crack cocaine and PCP.

## Marijuana adversely affects users' health.

Because users prefer to smoke marijuana, they expose themselves to many of the same health problems suffered by cigarette smokers. According to the ONDCP:

> Puff for puff, the amount of tar inhaled and the level of carbon monoxide absorbed by those who smoke marijuana, regardless of THC content, are three to five times greater than among tobacco smokers.

Consequently, people who use marijuana on a regular basis often have the same breathing problems as tobacco users, such as chronic coughing and wheezing, more frequent acute chest illnesses, and a tendency toward obstructed airways.[6]

Marijuana use has also been linked to other problems, including damage to the immune system, heart, lungs, and reproductive organs. In addition, the Drug Abuse Warning Network (DAWN) estimated that in 2002, marijuana was a contributing factor in more than 119,000 emergency room visits in the United States.

Marijuana poses a more serious risk to young people than it does to adults. The Canadian Senate committee that recommended that the drug be legalized nevertheless defined any marijuana use by a person under 16 as "at-risk" use, meaning that it puts the user in danger of becoming dependent. The drug's popularity among those of high school and college age is a serious concern because it interferes with learning ability. A study conducted at McLean Hospital in Massachusetts found that college students who regularly used marijuana suffered from impaired attention, memory, and learning for 24 hours after they last used the drug. Another study, conducted at the University of Iowa, found that frequent users of marijuana suffered the loss of verbal and mathematical skills as well impairment of their memory-retrieval processes. Studies have also found that the THC in marijuana attaches itself to receptors in the hippocampus region of the brain, weakening short-term memory and interfering with the mechanisms that form long-term memory.

Over time, we might discover that marijuana causes still more health problems. The World Health Organization says: "There are important gaps in knowledge about the health consequences of cannabis use which need to be addressed by well-controlled studies, including . . . the chronic adverse effects of cannabis use."[7] That is especially true because marijuana has become much more potent as the result of techniques such as cloning cannabis plants and feeding them high-nutrient fertilizers. According to the ONDCP: "Average THC levels rose from less than 1 percent in the mid-1970s to more than 6 percent in 2002. Sinsemilla [very high-grade marijuana] potency increased in the past two decades from 6 percent to more than 13 percent, with some samples containing THC levels of up to 33 percent."[8] Some experts believe that potent marijuana is more likely to make the user dependent on the drug.

### Marijuana impairs driving ability.

A study reported in the *Annals of Emergency Medicine* in 2000 found that even a moderate dose of marijuana could impair driving performance. A study conducted by National Highway Traffic Safety Administration (NHTSA) and a Dutch university found that THC impaired a driver's ability to maintain a constant speed, stay in one's lane, and react to the speed of the car in front; and that even a relatively low dose of THC slowed reaction time. Another study, conducted on pilots, found that smoking marijuana affected their performance on a flight simulator as long as 24 hours afterward, even though the pilots did not feel that their ability to fly was still impaired.

Traffic crashes are the number-one cause of death for 15- through 20-year-olds, the very age group most likely to use marijuana. The U.S. Transportation Department said in 2003:

> Estimates based on Monitoring the Future and Census Bureau data also show that of the nearly 4 million high school seniors in the United States, approximately one in six (600,000) drive under the influence of marijuana, a number nearly equivalent to those who drive under the influence of alcohol (640,000). Additionally, an estimated 38,000 of these students reported in 2001

*(continues on page 36)*

## FROM THE BENCH

*Board of Education of Independent School District No. 92 of Pottawatomie County v. Earls*, 536 U.S. 822 (2002)

The Fourth Amendment to the U.S. Constitution prohibits unreasonable searches and seizures. In general, the government must have at least some suspicion of wrongdoing before it can search a person. Drug tests, which have become commonplace in recent years, are considered "searches" if they are performed by government officials such as school administrators.

School boards in some communities became so concerned about drug use by students that they instituted drug-testing programs. In an effort to minimize Fourth Amendment concerns, testing was limited to students involved in extracurricular activities. School officials reasoned that since these activities were a "privilege," students could be made to comply with certain conditions—including remaining drug-free—in order to take part.

A school district in Oklahoma adopted a testing policy under which "students are required to take a drug test before participating in an extracurricular activity, must submit to random drug testing while participating in that activity, and must agree to be tested at any time upon reasonable suspicion. The urinalysis tests are designed to detect only the use of illegal drugs, including amphetamines, marijuana, cocaine, opiates, and barbiturates."

Lindsay Earls, who participated in several activities, challenged the school district's testing program. Her appeal reached the U.S. Supreme Court, which, in *Board of Education of Independent School District No. 92 of Pottawatomie County v. Earls*, upheld its constitutionality.

The vote was 5-to-4. Justice Clarence Thomas wrote the Court's opinion:

A student's privacy interest is limited in a public school environment where the State is responsible for maintaining discipline, health, and safety. Schoolchildren are routinely required to submit to physical examinations and vaccinations against disease.... Securing order in the school environment sometimes requires that students be subjected to greater controls than those appropriate for adults....

[T]he need to prevent and deter the substantial harm of childhood drug use provides the necessary immediacy for a school testing policy. Indeed, it would make little sense to require a school district to wait for a substantial portion of its students to begin using drugs before it was allowed to institute a drug testing program designed to deter drug use.

Given the nationwide epidemic of drug use, and the evidence of increased drug use in Tecumseh schools, it was entirely reasonable for the School District to enact this particular drug testing policy. . . .

In upholding the constitutionality of the Policy, we express no opinion as to its wisdom. Rather, we hold only that Tecumseh's Policy is a reasonable means of furthering the School District's important interest in preventing and deterring drug use among its schoolchildren.

Justice Stephen Breyer provided the fifth vote needed to make a majority. He agreed for the most part with Thomas's reasoning, but added:

In respect to the school's need for the drug testing program, I would emphasize the following: First, the drug problem in our Nation's schools is serious in terms of size, the kinds of drugs being used, and the consequences of that use both for our children and the rest of us. . . .

Second, the government's emphasis upon supply side interdiction apparently has not reduced teenage use in recent years. . . .

Third, public school systems must find effective ways to deal with this problem. Today's public expects its schools not simply to teach the fundamentals, but 'to shoulder the burden of feeding students breakfast and lunch, offering before and after school child care services, and providing medical and psychological services,' all in a school environment that is safe and encourages learning. . . .

Fourth, the program at issue here seeks to discourage demand for drugs by changing the school's environment in order to combat the single most important factor leading school children to take drugs, namely, peer pressure.

In her dissenting opinion, Justice Ruth Bader Ginsburg argued that the drug-testing problem was unconstitutional as well as counterproductive:

The particular testing program upheld today is not reasonable, it is capricious, even perverse: Petitioners' policy targets for testing a student population least likely to be at risk from illicit drugs and their damaging effects. . . .

*(continues)*

*(continued)*

Nationwide, students who participate in extracurricular activities are significantly less likely to develop substance abuse problems than are their less-involved peers.... Even if students might be deterred from drug use in order to preserve their extracurricular eligibility, it is at least as likely that other students might forgo their extracurricular involvement in order to avoid detection of their drug use. Tecumseh's policy thus falls short doubly if deterrence is its aim: It invades the privacy of students who need deterrence least, and risks steering students at greatest risk for substance abuse away from extracurricular involvement that potentially may palliate drug problems.

Note: Even though the student drug testing is permissible under the U.S. Constitution, some state constitutions provide broader privacy protection. One of those states is Washington. In 2008, that state's highest court unanimously ruled in *York v. Wahkiakum School District*, 163 Wash.2d 297, 178 P.3d 995 (Sup. Ct. 2008) that a school district's testing policy was an unconstitutional invasion of privacy.

*(continued from page 33)*

that they crashed while driving under the influence of marijuana and 46,000 reported that they crashed while driving under the influence of alcohol.[9]

Making the problem worse yet is the practice, common among young people at parties, of using marijuana and alcohol together. The Canadian Senate panel found that "[a] significant percentage of impaired drivers test positive for cannabis and alcohol together. The effects of cannabis when combined with alcohol are more significant than is the case for alcohol alone."[10] The panel went on to recommend reducing by half the maximum allowable blood-alcohol concentration for drivers who had consumed both alcohol and other drugs.

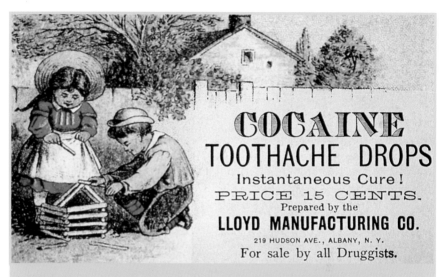

COCAINE
TOOTHACHE DROPS

Instantaneous Cure!
PRICE 15 CENTS.
Prepared by the

LLOYD MANUFACTURING CO.
219 HUDSON AVE., ALBANY, N. Y.
For sale by all Druggists.

A late nineteenth-century advertisement for Cocaine Toothache Drops promises to be an "Instantaneous Cure!" While the ad may seem ridiculous by today's standards, this is only due to the fact that society's knowledge of cocaine's dangers has increased since then. At the time, the drug's benefits in relieving pain made it both legal and appreciated.

### Medical marijuana does more harm than good.

Opponents of medical marijuana point to a landmark study by the Institute of Medicine (IOM), released in 1999, which concluded that "smoked marijuana is a crude drug delivery system that exposes patients to a significant number of harmful substances."[11] Furthermore, many in the medical community oppose the use of smoked marijuana as medicine. The American Medical Association favors keeping marijuana on Schedule I of controlled substances until more research is done; and both the American Cancer Society and the National Multiple Sclerosis Society have serious reservations about the drug's effectiveness.

Medical marijuana also undermines a regulatory framework, built over many decades, that protects Americans from dangerous and ineffective medications. The Food and Drug Administration (FDA), which regulates potential new drugs, says:

> FDA's drug approval process requires well-controlled clinical trials that provide the necessary scientific data upon which FDA makes its approval and labeling decisions. . . . Efforts that seek to bypass the FDA drug approval process would not serve the interests of public health because they might expose patients to unsafe and ineffective drug products. FDA has not approved smoked marijuana for any condition or disease indication.[12]

Whether a drug is safe and effective should be determined by the scientific method, not popular vote.

Furthermore, medical marijuana is a thinly disguised first step toward legalization. In 2004, Ethan Nadelmann, the head of the Drug Policy Alliance, said on MSNBC: "As medical marijuana becomes more regulated and institutionalized in the West, that may provide a model for how we ultimately make marijuana legal for all adults."[13] Medical-marijuana laws hamper the police by diverting medical marijuana into the recreational drug market, and by complicating the job of law enforcement by forcing officers to distinguish medical users from recreational users. These laws also appear to have made the drug more socially acceptable. The 1999 National Household Survey on Drug Abuse found that those states that had medical marijuana laws were among the highest in levels of past-month marijuana use. Opponents also contend that legalizing medical marijuana would lead to use of the drug in the workplace and add to the number of people who drive while under the influence of marijuana.

Finally, it appears that medical marijuana is being used by a large number of patients who are not suffering from cancer or some other serious illness for which the drug was legalized as a "last-resort" form of treatment. Although California's medical-marijuana law contains a list of conditions that qualify for medical marijuana, that list also includes a loophole—"any other illness for which marijuana provides relief." Critics argue that this enables doctors to recommend the drug for almost any ailment. A recent survey of some 2,500 patients, conducted by Dr. Tod Mikuriya, found that almost three-quarters used marijuana for pain relief or mental health problems.

## Summary

Government has the power to protect citizens from dangerous substances. Today, marijuana is illegal because studies show that it is dangerous to users as well as society. A growing number of users have become dependent on it, and many need treatment to break their dependence. Users may suffer other health problems, especially damage to the lungs caused by marijuana smoke. Marijuana has been linked to traffic crashes, crime and delinquency, and progression to hard drugs. Young people, who account for many of the nation's current marijuana users, are still developing physically and mentally. For that reason they are especially vulnerable to the marijuana's harmful effects. In recent years, highly potent strains of marijuana have appeared on the market, raising the possibility of even more serious problems in the future.

# Marijuana Does Not Cause Serious Harm

Supporters of current policy say that marijuana is illegal because it is dangerous. A series of government-commissioned studies, however, have come to the conclusion that marijuana is less dangerous than people are led to believe. In 1972, the Shafer Commission concluded that marijuana use at its then-level did not constitute a major threat to public health. Nearly 40 years later, a study by a committee of the Canadian Senate concluded that used in moderation, marijuana in itself posed very little danger to users or to society as a whole.

Nevertheless, marijuana remains prohibited in the United States and hundreds of thousands of people are arrested every year for using it. Even though the Obama administration's National Drug Control Strategy, announced in May 2010, treats the use of illegal drugs—including marijuana—more as a public-health problem than previous administrations have, arrest data indicate that law-enforcement agencies are still vigorously enforcing laws against marijuana use.

## Our marijuana policy is based on fear.

Early marijuana laws were prompted in large part by ignorance and racial prejudice. Often laws were passed with little debate, let alone input from the medical and scientific communities. For example, Congress passed the Marijuana Tax Act in 1937 even though there was no medical testimony in favor of it. In fact, the only doctor who showed up to testify spoke against the legislation. A panel of the National Academy of Sciences found that over the years, marijuana has been blamed for a variety of harm to society: "in the 1930s, provoking crime and violence; in the early 1950s, leading to heroin addiction; and in the late 1960s, making people passive, lowering motivation and productivity, and destroying the American work ethic in young people."[1]

The latest example of fearmongering involves "potent pot." As head of the Office of National Drug Control Policy, John Walters warned parents that modern marijuana was 10 to 20 times as potent as the marijuana they may have used when they were young. In fact, a federally funded study found that the THC content had only doubled, from 2 percent to 4.2 percent, between 1980 and 2000. Furthermore, users can adjust to higher-potency marijuana. Mark Kleiman, a professor at the University of California, Los Angeles, says that more potent marijuana does not mean more highly intoxicated users: "The line for marijuana is flat as a pancake. Kids who get stoned today aren't getting any more stoned than their parents were. That ought to be the end of the argument."[2]

From the beginning, scare tactics has gone hand in hand with tough laws and aggressive enforcement. During the 1930s, Harry Anslinger warned of "wide and increasing abuse" of "this lethal weed," and helped place articles with titles such as "Marijuana Assassin of Youth" in popular magazines. Anti-marijuana propaganda reached its peak with the appearance of *Reefer Madness*, a sensationalistic film aimed at parents. Its depiction of the dangers of marijuana was so extreme that college students showed it as a cult film during the 1970s. Even in this century, the government resorts to scare tactics, such as the "box cutter" ad linking drug use to terrorism that ran during the Super Bowl just months after the September 11, 2001, terrorist attacks. Some advocates, such as Marsha Rosenbaum, argue that these campaigns do more harm than good:

## THE LETTER OF THE LAW

## California's Compassionate Use Act of 1996, *California Health & Safety Code* §11362.5

In 1996, California became the first state in the modern era to legalize the use of marijuana for medical purposes when voters approved Proposition 215, the Compassionate Use Act. The act reads as follows:

(a) This section shall be known and may be cited as the Compassionate Use Act of 1996.

(b)(1) The people of the State of California hereby find and declare that the purposes of the Compassionate Use Act of 1996 are as follows:

    (A) To ensure that seriously ill Californians have the right to obtain and use marijuana for medical purposes where that medical use is deemed appropriate and has been recommended by a physician who has determined that the person's health would benefit from the use of marijuana in the treatment of cancer, anorexia, AIDS, chronic pain, spasticity, glaucoma, arthritis, migraine, or any other illness for which marijuana provides relief.

    (B) To ensure that patients and their primary caregivers who obtain and use marijuana for medical purposes upon the recommendation of a physician are not subject to criminal prosecution or sanction.

    (C) To encourage the federal and state governments to implement a plan to provide for the safe and affordable distribution of marijuana to all patients in medical need of marijuana.

[T]he consistent mischaracterization of marijuana may be the Achilles' heel of current drug prevention approaches because programs and messages too often contain exaggerations and misinformation that contradict young people's own observations and experience. As a result, teens become cynical and lose confidence in what we, as parents and teachers, tell them.[3]

(2) Nothing in this section shall be construed to supersede legislation prohibiting persons from engaging in conduct that endangers others, nor to condone the diversion of marijuana for nonmedical purposes.

(c) Notwithstanding any other provision of law, no physician in this state shall be punished, or denied any right or privilege, for having recommended marijuana to a patient for medical purposes.

(d) Section 11357, relating to the possession of marijuana, and Section 11358, relating to the cultivation of marijuana, shall not apply to a patient, or to a patient's primary caregiver, who possesses or cultivates marijuana for the personal medical purposes of the patient upon the written or oral recommendation or approval of a physician.

(e) For the purposes of this section, "primary caregiver" means the individual designated by the person exempted under this section who has consistently assumed responsibility for the housing, health, or safety of that person.

In 2003, California lawmakers passed legislation (Chapter 875, Statutes of 2003, codified as *California Health & Safety Code* §§11362.7-11362.83) that attempted to address "problems and uncertainties" concerning the Compassionate Use Act, especially arrests of medical-marijuana patients and their caregivers. The legislation created a statewide registry of patients and caregivers, and gave them the right to apply for identification cards that they could show to police officers if they are stopped. It also exempted marijuana "co-operatives" that distribute the drug to patients (federal law still prohibits co-operatives) from prosecution, and allows patients to possess up to eight ounces of marijuana and keep up to six mature cannabis plants.

### Few marijuana users suffer serious harm.

One of the most terrifying dangers of using illegal drugs is the possibility of dying from an overdose, yet it is virtually impossible to die as the result of smoking too much marijuana. A federal administrative law judge found in 1988:

> Nearly all medicines have toxic, potentially lethal effects. But marijuana is not such a substance. There is no record in the extensive medical literature describing a proven, documented cannabis-induced fatality.
>
> This is a remarkable statement. First, the record on marijuana encompasses 5,000 years of human experience. Second, marijuana is now used daily by enormous numbers of people throughout the world.[4]

On the other hand, many thousands of Americans have died from using legal medications. An analysis of Food and Drug Administration (FDA) data by ProCon.org found that a sample of FDA-approved medications—which included anti-psychotics, attention-deficit disorder (ADD) medications, painkillers, and other prescription drugs—were suspected as the primary cause of 10,008 deaths and as a secondary cause in 1,679 more in a single period of study. By contrast, marijuana was the primary suspect in zero deaths and a suspected secondary factor in 279 deaths.

The danger associated with taking any drug depends on how it is used, not whether it is legal. In the case of marijuana, the Shafer Commission found "little proven danger" of physical or psychological harm from "the experimental or intermittent use of natural marijuana," and added that the real danger came from "heavy, long-term use of the drug, particularly of the most potent preparations."[5] Most people, however, never become heavy, long-term users.

Some risks of using marijuana are of particular interest to young people and their parents. One is the possibility of a psychotic reaction to the drug. That danger, however, has been exaggerated. The Canadian Senate committee found that "[n]o mental pathology directly related to the overuse of cannabis has been reported, which distinguishes this substance from psychostimulants such as [Ecstasy], cocaine or alcohol, heavy and repeated use of which can give rise to characteristic psychotic syndromes."[6] A leading textbook on substance abuse states that so-called "panic attacks" are uncommon, and that simple reassurance is the best method of treating them.

Another risk is the "amotivational syndrome," the loss of interest in virtually all activities except getting high on marijuana. Lack of motivation is a legitimate concern, especially for parents of high school and college students who use the drug. The Canadian Senate panel, however, found that most studies ruled out this syndrome as a consequence of using marijuana. Studies conducted in Jamaica, Costa Rica, and Greece found no evidence that even heavy long-term users suffered intellectual or neurological damage, changes in personality, or loss of the will to work or participate in society. It has been theorized that people who are bored, depressed, or alienated to begin with turn to marijuana as an excuse for failure, or use it as a form of self-medication.

## Marijuana does not make users drug addicts or criminals.

The World Health Organization defines addiction as "the repeated use of a psychoactive substance to the extent the user is periodically or chronically intoxicated, shows a compulsion to take the preferred substance, has great difficulty in voluntarily ceasing or modifying substance use, and exhibits determination to obtain the substance by almost any means."[7] Few marijuana users meet that definition. In fact, nearly everybody who tries marijuana eventually gives it up—which would be almost impossible if the drug were highly addictive.

Although people become dependent on marijuana, the Canadian Senate committee found that only 10 percent to 20 percent of regular users meet the criteria for dependence. The committee also observed: "What form does cannabis dependency take? Most authors agree that psychological dependency on cannabis is relatively minor. In fact, it cannot be compared in any way with tobacco or alcohol dependency and is even less common than dependency on certain psychotropic medications."[8] Furthermore, most marijuana users stop using the drug without going into treatment. Critics of marijuana prohibition point out that most people who seek treatment for marijuana dependence are also dependent on other drugs, such as cocaine or alcohol. They also contend that many marijuana users are sent to treatment by the criminal justice system or their families—regardless of whether they meet the criteria for dependence.

Supporters of current policy warn that marijuana almost inevitably leads to harder drugs. That statement is based on statistics showing that most hard drug users had tried marijuana as their first illegal substance. This, however, is faulty reasoning. The fact that marijuana users are more likely to use hard drugs does not mean marijuana *causes* them to do so. One factor that leads to hard drug use is a tendency to take risks. Those who are drawn to high-risk behavior, such as taking up dangerous sports or engaging in unprotected sex, are more likely to gravitate to the most dangerous drugs. Another factor is the company a person keeps. People who use illegal drugs are more likely to find themselves in situations where those drugs are available. They are also more likely to consider themselves "outlaws," which make the use of harder drugs more likely.

If marijuana is a "gateway" drug, then so are alcohol and tobacco, both of which are legal. In 1999, the Institute of Medicine found:

> In the sense that marijuana use typically precedes rather than follows initiation of other illicit drug use, it is indeed a "gateway" drug. But because underage smoking and alcohol use typically precede marijuana use, marijuana is not the most common, and is rarely the

first, "gateway" to illicit drug use. There is no conclusive evidence that the drug effects of marijuana are causally linked to the subsequent abuse of other illicit drugs.[9]

In addition, the assertion that many heroin users started with marijuana fails to account for the vast majority of marijuana users who never progress to heroin.

From the time marijuana first appeared in the United States, it has been blamed for causing users to commit crime. Although marijuana use is more common among those who have been arrested, this finding does not prove that marijuana causes people to break the law. To begin with, there are no known chemicals in marijuana that cause the user to commit crimes. As the Shafer Commission found:

> Laboratory studies provide no evidence that marijuana produces effects which can be interpreted as crimino-genic. . . . The original relationship [between marijuana and crime] is usually found to derive not from the chemical effects of the drug but from the operation of social and cultural variables unrelated to either the drug or its use.[10]

Experts point out that marijuana use induces a mild lethargy that is not conducive to physical activity, let alone criminal acts. Marijuana users are much less likely than hard-drug users to act violently while under the influence, or to steal in order to get money to buy the drug. Furthermore, the argument that marijuana puts the user on a path to crime confuses cause and effect. A person who starts breaking the law at an early age is more likely to be exposed to illegal drugs, experiment with them, and begin a career as a drug user.

## Marijuana is less harmful than some legal drugs.

Alcohol and tobacco are legal, but these drugs are both deadly and costly. Every year, alcohol-related traffic crashes kill some 17,000

Americans, and alcohol is responsible for more than 20,000 non-traffic-related deaths. Studies cited by the National Institute of Alcohol Abuse and Alcoholism estimate that alcohol costs this

## FROM THE BENCH

### *Ravin v. State,* 537 P. 2d 494 (Alaska 1975)

In 1972, the Shafer Commission recommended that penalties for private posses-sion and use of marijuana be eliminated. Neither Congress nor any state legisla-ture followed that recommendation; as of 2009, only 11 states had eliminated criminal penalties for possessing or using small amounts. Alaska is one of those states. In *Ravin v. State*, that state's highest court effectively legalized the posses-sion and use of marijuana by adults in their own home.

The case began when Irwin Ravin was arrested for possession of marijuana. Ravin raised two constitutional challenges to his arrest. First, Alaska's marijuana law violated the privacy rights of adults who possessed marijuana for their per-sonal use; and second, classifying marijuana as a dangerous drug, while allowing the possession of alcohol and tobacco, denied him equal protection of the law.

The court rejected Ravin's equal-protection claim and upheld the classification of marijuana as a dangerous drug. It did agree, however, with Ravin's privacy claim. Here are excerpts from Justice Jay Rabinowitz's majority opinion:

> If there is any area of human activity to which a right to privacy pertains more than any other, it is the home. . . .
>
> The state is under no obligation to allow otherwise "private" activity which will result in numbers of people becoming public charges or other-wise burdening the public welfare. But we do not find that such a situation exists today regarding marijuana. It appears that the effects of marijuana on the individual are not serious enough to justify widespread concern, at least as compared with the far more dangerous effects of alcohol, barbiturates and amphetamines. . . .
>
> The state has a legitimate concern with avoiding the spread of mari-juana use to adolescents . . . as well as a legitimate concern with the prob-lem of driving under the influence of marijuana. Yet these interests are insufficient to justify intrusions into the rights of adults in the privacy of their own homes. . . .
>
> In view of our holding that possession of marijuana by adults at home for personal use is constitutionally protected, we wish to make clear that we

country between $140 billion and $230 billion a year. According to the Centers for Disease Control and Prevention, smoking is responsible for 440,000 deaths per year, and costs more than $190

do not mean to condone the use of marijuana. . . . It is the responsibility of every individual to consider carefully the ramifications for himself and for those around him of using such substances.

Some supporters of decriminalization thought the *Ravin* decision was the start of a trend. No other state court, however, followed Alaska's lead. For example, in *State v. Mallan*, 86 Hawaii 440, 950 P. 2d 178 (1998), the Supreme Court of Hawaii rejected Lloyd Mallan's contention that the state Constitution's guarantee of privacy gave him the right to possess and use marijuana for recreational purposes. Justice Robert Klein's majority opinion, which discussed earlier privacy decisions at some length, rejected Mallan's argument. He wrote:

In the present case, Mallan argues that the right to privacy in article I, section 6 encompasses the right to possess marijuana for personal use. We disagree. . . . It is clear that the right to possess and use marijuana cannot be considered a "fundamental" right. . . . In Hawaii, possession of marijuana has been illegal since 1931. . . . In the rest of the United States, the possession and/or use of marijuana, even in small quantities, is almost universally prohibited. Therefore, tradition appears to be in favor of the prohibition against possession and use of marijuana. Additionally, we have no reason to believe that the collective conscience of the people supports the possession and use of marijuana under the circumstances of this case. Furthermore, we cannot say that the principles of liberty and justice underlying our civil and political institutions are violated by marijuana possession laws. We dare say that liberty and justice can exist in spite of the prohibition against marijuana possession.

*A postscript.* Many Alaskans disagreed with the *Ravin* decision because they objected to judges "legislating from the bench" and were concerned that it would result in an increase in marijuana use, especially by young people. There have been two attempts to overturn the decision: a statewide referendum in 1990, and an act of the state legislature in 2006. The Supreme Court of Alaska, however, has not yet ruled that either of these actions actually changed the state Constitution, so *Ravin* is believed to be a good law, at least for now.

billion a year in health care costs and lost productivity. The costs attributable to using marijuana are much lower. A Canadian study reported in 2009 in the *British Columbia Mental Health and Addictions Journal* found that the health-related costs of

## THE LETTER OF THE LAW

### Title II, Comprehensive Drug Abuse Prevention and Control Act of 1970 (Public Law 91-513), codified as 21 U.S.C. §§801 and following

The Controlled Substances Act took effect in 1970. It was part of an overhaul of the nation's narcotics laws. The act's most important feature was a classification system, under which drugs were assigned to "schedules" with varying levels of regulation. In assigning drugs to a schedule, the CSA directs the federal government to consider the following:

(1) The drug's actual or relative potential for abuse.

(2) Scientific evidence of its known effect on the human body.

(3) The state of current scientific knowledge of the drug.

(4) Its history and current pattern of abuse.

(5) The scope, duration, and significance of abuse.

(6) What risk, if any, the drug poses to public health.

(7) The risk that users will become physically or psychologically dependent on it.

(8) Whether the drug is used, or is likely to be used, to produce a substance already controlled under the act.

Two federal departments, the Department of Justice and the Department of Health and Human Services, which receive input from the Food and Drug Administration, determine which drugs are added to or removed from the various schedules.

Cannabis, which includes marijuana and hashish, was placed in Schedule I, the most heavily regulated category, and has remained there ever since. Drugs in Schedule I—which also include heroin, Ecstasy, LSD, and mescaline—have no recognized medical use, and may not be prescribed by doctors.

marijuana use were $20 per user, compared with $165 per alcohol user and more than $800 per tobacco user.

In 2007, a British panel of experts ranked 20 drugs, legal and illegal, based on the physical harm they caused to the individual

---

The CSA contains four other schedules:

- *Schedule II.* These drugs are available by prescription only. The category includes cocaine, Ritalin, opium, oxycodone (the main ingredient in the pain relievers Percocet and OxyContin), morphine, and amphetamine (a drug that stimulates the central nervous system).

- *Schedule III.* These are also available by prescription only, but controls on distribution and prescription refills are less stringent than for Schedule II drugs. The category includes anabolic steroids (compounds that grow and repair human tissue, but are sometimes used by athletes to increase their size and strength), and the pain relievers Vicodin and Tylenol 3.

- *Schedule IV.* The amount of regulation for this category of drugs is similar to Schedule III. It includes tranquilizers such as Xanax, Librium, and Valium, and the sleep aid Ambien.

- *Schedule V.* Some drugs in this schedule are available without a prescription. The category includes drugs with small amounts of opium or codeine, such as some cough suppressants.

The CSA has been criticized for classification decisions that do not reflect actual danger. As David Musto, a professor at Yale Medical School, wrote:

The history of drug laws in the United States shows that the degree to which a drug has been outlawed or curbed has no direct relation to its inherent danger. . . . Establishing actual dangerousness sounds reasonable, but the process had its difficulties. If the dangers of drugs were to be ranked according to deaths linked to their use, tobacco and alcohol would head the list. These substances, however, had powerful economic and political interests behind them and moreover were not part of the public's fear over the drug crisis.*

*David F. Musto, *The American Disease: Origins of Narcotic Control.* New York: Oxford University Press, 1987, p. 260.

A group of hippies are shown gathering at Hyde Park in London, England, on July 5, 1969 to hear The Rolling Stones in a free five-hour concert. Marijuana use among young people increased in the 1960s and 1970s.

user, their tendency to cause dependence, and overall harm to society. The experts found that the legal classification often had little relationship to how potentially harmful a drug was. The eight drugs they ranked as most dangerous included two that were not even listed in that country's Misuse of Drugs Act. Professor Colin Blakemore, the co-author of the study, said: "Alcohol and tobacco are way up there in the league table, not far behind heroin and cocaine and street methadone. Society has not only come to terms with alcohol and tobacco but is well aware of the harms associated with them so we felt it was useful to include them as calibration points for other drugs."[11]

Some draw a parallel between marijuana and caffeine. When the drug was first introduced into Europe, there was a move to suppress it. The medical community warned that caffeine was addictive. That statement is literally true: Caffeine users develop a tolerance for the drug, and suffer withdrawal symptoms if they stop taking it. Caffeine is also poisonous to those who consume too much of it. Caffeine, however, is not only legal but widely accepted in society. The editors of *Consumer Reports* explains:

> The answer is quite simple. Coffee, tea, cocoa, and the cola drinks have been *domesticated*. Caffeine has been incorporated into our way of life in a manner that minimizes (though it does not altogether eliminate) the hazards inherent in caffeine use. Instead of its being classified as an illicit drug, thereby grossly amplifying caffeine's potential for harm, ways to make caffeine safer have been searched for and found.[12]

They add that caffeine prohibition would have pushed users to the margins of society and given rise to a black market in the drug—as is the case with other illegal drugs. There are signs that we are "domesticating" marijuana. In 1982, a National Academy of Sciences panel observed that moderation is encouraged when a drug is introduced gradually; that is, to a growing population of users, as with marijuana in the 1960s and early 1970s.

## Summary

Fear, ignorance, and prejudice all played a part in making marijuana illegal in the United States, and our government still uses fear to discourage use of the drug. Even though penalties for using marijuana are less severe than they once were, many Americans believe they are still too strict and some think lawmakers have exaggerated marijuana's dangers. By and large, the drug is not addictive and does not lead to the use of "harder" drugs or cause its users to become criminals. There is evidence that marijuana is less harmful than alcohol, tobacco, and some over-the-counter medications. Government commissions in the United States and elsewhere that have studied marijuana generally agree that the drug is less dangerous than public officials say it is.

# Marijuana Should Remain Illegal

Opponents of the United States's marijuana policy believe that using the drug is a "victimless crime" that should not be punished. They argue that government has no business regulating private behavior. Supporters of the laws disagree. They insist that marijuana use affects nonusers, who have to live with marijuana-related crime and pay the costs of abuse of the drug. They also argue that marijuana use is contrary to the notion of personal responsibility. The Shafer Commission pointed out that society can—and does—legislate against behavior it finds offensive:

> If society feels strongly enough about the impropriety of
> a certain behavior, it may choose to utilize the criminal
> law even though the behavior is largely invisible and will
> be minimized only through effective operation of other

agencies of social control. Laws against incest and child-beating are good examples.[1]

## Americans support the current policy.

Opinion polls show that a majority of Americans favor keeping marijuana illegal. In 2004, voters in Alaska and Nevada defeated ballot proposals that would have allowed adults to use marijuana. In both states, the ratio of defeat was better than 3-to-2. There are several reasons why the public opposes legalization. One is that most people still object to marijuana, even though millions of Americans use the drug and tens of millions more have tried it. When marijuana became popular during the 1960s, it was widely associated with a lifestyle that many Americans found offensive. The Shafer Commission found:

> Use of the drug is linked with idleness, lack of motivation, hedonism and sexual promiscuity. Many see the drug as fostering a counterculture which conflicts with basic moral precepts as well as with the operating functions of our society. The "dropping out" or rejection of the established value system is viewed with alarm. Marijuana becomes more than a drug; it becomes a symbol of the rejection of cherished values.[2]

This way of life offends most Americans who still subscribe to a "work ethic"—in other words, a belief that work is good in its own right and that each of us has an obligation to make the most of our talents. For that reason, marijuana users are often thought of as lazy and lacking ambition.

If marijuana were legalized despite the majority's desire to prohibit it, many would consider the new policy a surrender to a law-breaking minority. The Shafer Commission observed that obedience of the law was "highly valued" in our society, and that remains true today. Although lawmakers sometimes pass legislation that many citizens staunchly oppose—the civil rights laws of the 1960s are an example—they do so only when upholding a fundamental principle justifies it. No such principle supports legalizing marijuana. Furthermore, an abrupt change in the law could generate a backlash. Our experience with the legal drinking age provides an example of what can happen when the law is changed too quickly. During the 1970s, many states lowered the age of majority from 21 to 18. Literally overnight, thousands of young adults were able to drink legally. Unfortunately, many of them had never been taught how to drink responsibly. Within a few years, a sharp increase in alcohol-related traffic crashes among young drivers prompted lawmakers to raise the drinking age back to 21.

Making matters worse is that our society has no experience with legal marijuana. As a result, marijuana is on a different footing than alcohol, which the United States prohibited between 1920 and 1933. As the Shafer Commission explained:

> With marijuana . . . the prevailing policy of eliminating use had never been opposed to any significant degree until the mid-1960's. Unlike the prohibition of alcohol, which had been the subject of public debate off and on for 60 years before it was adopted, present marijuana policy has not until now engaged the public opinion process, some 50 years after it first began to be used. Majority sentiment does not appear to be as flexible as it was with alcohol.[3]

Finally, some experts believe that ending marijuana prohibition would open the door to widespread irresponsible use. The editors of *Consumer Reports* warned: "A nation that has not learned to keep away from some drugs and to use others wisely cannot be taught those essential lessons merely by repealing drug laws."[4] That same year, the Shafer Commission said: "While continuing concern about the effects of heavy, chronic use is not sufficient reason to maintain an overly harsh public policy, it is still a significant argument for choosing official discouragement in preference to official neutrality."[5] During the late 1970s, when marijuana was a low priority for law enforcement, usage rates reached an all-time high, especially among young people.

## Marijuana use harms others.

Because marijuana use impairs driving ability, it adds to the risk of nonusers being killed or injured in traffic crashes. Marijuana use at work generates costs the rest of society has to pay. The National Institute on Drug Abuse cites a study of postal workers which found that employees who tested positive for marijuana on a pre-employment drug test had 55 percent more industrial accidents, 85 percent more injuries, and 75 percent more absenteeism compared with those who tested negative. Marijuana users are also less productive at work. In addition, society has to pay the cost of treating people with marijuana dependence and for medical care for those who get injured while under the influence.

Marijuana use helps fund organized criminals. The Latin American Commission on Drugs and Democracy said: "The relationship between homicide, firearm and drug commerce is central. Drugs finance the purchase of firearms, which sustain gang wars for control of territories and trafficking. The geography of drug and arms trafficking does not respect national sovereignties or borders."[6] The commission also said: "The illegal firearms market, generally linked with drug sales, is the major culprit in the high rate of homicides particularly among youth. Even though violence and lack of security affect all citizens, homicide rates are significantly higher in low-income districts and where city services are most deficient."[7]

Marijuana use even damages the environment. Much of the marijuana produced in America is grown on public lands, including our national forests and parks. The Office of National Drug Control Policy says:

According to officers with the Forest Service and other agencies, many of California's illegal marijuana fields are controlled ... by employees of Mexican drug-trafficking organizations carrying high-powered assault weapons. During the growing season, the officers say, the cartels smuggle hundreds of undocumented Mexican

## The DEA Says "No" to Reclassifying Marijuana

When Congress passed the Controlled Substances Act in 1970, it placed marijuana in Schedule I, which means that it has no legitimate medical use and can be used only in research projects approved by the federal government. Since then, there have been several attempts to have marijuana moved into a less restrictive schedule so that doctors may be able to prescribe it.

Shortly after the CSA became law, advocates of medical marijuana petitioned the Drug Enforcement Administration to take marijuana out of Schedule I so that doctors could prescribe it. The petition languished at the DEA for years on account of political opposition to even debating marijuana's merits. After a long legal battle, the DEA finally held hearings on medical marijuana. In 1988, administrative law judge Francis Young issued an opinion (*In the Matter of Marijuana Rescheduling Petition*, Drug Enforcement Administration Docket No. 86–22 [September 6, 1988]) in which he recommended that the drug be moved to Schedule II. The DEA, however, rejected the judge's findings and left marijuana in Schedule I.

In 1995, Jon Gettman filed another petition with the DEA, again asking that marijuana be rescheduled. Six years later, after examining the scientific and medical evidence, the DEA turned down Gettman's petition. Here are excerpts from the DEA's Notice of Denial of Petition (*Federal Register*, vol. 66, no. 76, pp. 20038-20076 [April 18, 2001]):

> The weight of the scientific and medical evidence ... supports the three findings that (1) Marijuana has a high potential for abuse, (2) marijuana has no currently accepted medical use in the United States, and (3) there is a lack of accepted evidence about the safety of using marijuana under medical supervision. . . .

nationals into the U.S. to work the fields, bringing with them pesticides, equipment, and guns.[8]

Finally, most Americans believe the law should prevent people from engaging in dangerous behavior. That is why, for example, many states require motorcyclists to wear helmets. The

Throughout his petition, Mr. Gettman argues that while many people "use" marijuana, few "abuse" it. He appears to equate abuse with the level of physical dependence and toxicity resulting from marijuana use.... The actual use and frequency of use of a substance ... are indicative of a substance's abuse potential....

Acute use of marijuana causes an impairment of psychomotor performance, including performance of complex tasks, which makes it inadvisable to operate motor vehicles or heavy equipment after using marijuana. People who have or are at risk of developing psychiatric disorders may be the most vulnerable to developing dependence on marijuana. Dysphoria [feelings of anxiety, restlessness, and depression] is a potential response in a minority of individuals who use marijuana....

Marijuana smoke is considered to be comparable to tobacco smoke in respect to increased risk of cancer, lung damage, and poor pregnancy outcome. An additional concern includes the potential for dependence on marijuana.

Individuals with Cannabis Dependence have compulsive use and assorted problems.... Individuals with Cannabis Dependence may also persist in their use despite knowledge of physical problems (e.g., chronic cough related to smoking) or psychological conditions (e.g., excessive sedation and a decrease in goal-oriented activities resulting from repeated use of high doses).

Gettman appealed the DEA's decision to the U.S. Court of Appeals for the District of Columbia Circuit, which dismissed the appeal on the grounds that he and his fellow petitioners were not sufficiently injured by the DEA's decision to have standing to challenge it.* Since 2001, several individuals have filed petitions asking the DEA to reschedule marijuana. The DEA, however, has refused to revisit the issue.

*Gettman v. Drug Enforcement, 290F.3d 430 (D.C.Cir. 2002).

theory behind these laws is that even if a person ignores the risk of death or injury, the possibility of getting arrested might provide enough incentive to avoid the risky activity. In any event, as a society we are not neutral, and the law reflects our desire to promote or discourage certain behavior. As one police official told the Canadian Senate committee: "When we have sanctions against drugs, it reduces social acceptability and helps hold consumption down. Two aspects of acceptability are perceived risk in using the drug and perceived social acceptance of the drug."[9]

## Marijuana penalties are proportional to the offense.

Supporters of more liberal marijuana laws often cite cases of people who are sentenced to lengthy prison terms for simple possession of the drug. ONDCP calls those accusations unfounded:

> Built into the criminal justice system is an appropriate measure of discretion that responds to the gravity of the offense. Those who persistently violate the country's drug laws face criminal penalties, which may include time behind bars. For offenders whose involvement in lawbreaking is minor, the sanctions are slight and often involve a referral to treatment rather than incarceration.[10]

In fact, few Americans are sent to prison for simple possession. In 1997, the Bureau of Justice Statistics (BJS) found that 0.7 percent of inmates in state prisons were there for marijuana offenses, and that less than half of them were there for a first offense of marijuana possession. The BJS also estimated that the median amount of marijuana possessed by those who went to prison was *115 pounds*—tens of thousands of times larger than a "personal-use" amount. Other factors that lead to a prison sentence include prior offenses; being caught with the drug while on probation or parole; or committing other crimes, such as illegally carrying a gun while possessing marijuana. Furthermore, many of those imprisoned for possession were originally charged with more serious offenses, such as trafficking, and pled guilty to the lesser charge of possession, with a prison term being part of the plea bargain.

Small-time offenders rarely go to jail, let alone prison. Eleven states specifically rule out jail time for first offenders caught with personal-use amounts—typically, less than an ounce; and even in states where possession remains a crime, jail sentences are uncommon. In fact, many first offenders—even those found with more than a personal-use amount—can avoid not only jail but a criminal record as well. The ONDCP explains:

> At least 23 states offer . . . plans offering deferred prosecution in exchange for a promise not to violate the terms of the probation. . . . But if the offender stays clean and commits no crimes for the prescribed time period, no further court appearance is necessary. The matter is settled, the police fingerprint file destroyed. No jail time, no criminal record—end of story.[11]

Finally, the DEA takes issue with critics who argue that we are spending too much of our resources on enforcing the nation's drug laws: "For example, in 2002, the amount of money spent by the federal government on drug control was less than $19 billion. And unlike critics of American drug policy would have you believe, all of those funds did not go to enforcement policy only. Those funds were used for treatment, education and prevention, as well as enforcement."[12]

To put this amount in perspective, the federal drug-control budget is not much larger than that for welfare or foreign aid, and far less than what the federal government spends on national defense or Social Security. The amount spent on enforcement is also much smaller than the economic impact of drug abuse, which is estimated to be $140 billion per year.

### Enforcement reduces crime and drug problems.

Even though prohibition has not eliminated all drug use, it nevertheless has been a success. The DEA explains:

> In 1880, many drugs, including opium and cocaine, were legal. . . . There were over 400,000 opium addicts in our nation. That's twice as many per capita as there are today. . . . But we fought those problems by passing and enforcing tough laws and by educating the public about the dangers of those drugs. And this vigilance

## FROM THE BENCH

### *United States v. Oakland Cannabis Buyers' Cooperative*, 523 U.S. 483 (2001)

Fourteen states have passed laws allowing patients to use marijuana if they suffer from conditions that cannot be helped by conventional medication and if a doctor has recommended marijuana. The legalization of "medical marijuana," however, spurred a long—and still unresolved—legal battle. The federal government insists on uniform enforcement of the Controlled Substances Act, which classifies marijuana is a Schedule I drug, meaning that doctors cannot prescribe it and patients cannot use it for any purpose.

After California legalized medical marijuana in 1996, federal authorities promptly took legal action against providers of the drug. The Justice Department filed suit against six co-operatives that supplied marijuana to patients. One of them, the Oakland Cannabis Buyers' Co-Operative, challenged the government's action in court. The cooperative operated openly and had the support of the city government. In court, the cooperative raised the defense of "medical necessity": if it did not provide marijuana, patients would unnecessarily suffer.

The appeal reached the U.S. Supreme Court, which, in *United States v. Oakland Cannabis Buyers' Cooperative*, unanimously rejected the cooperative's argument. Here are excerpts from Justice Clarence Thomas's majority opinion:

> Under any conception of a legal necessity, one principle is clear: The [medical necessity] defense cannot succeed when the legislature itself has made

worked—by World War II, drug use was reduced to the very margins of society.[13]

Although some have heavily criticized it, the "war on drugs" has made a difference. Illicit drug use reached its peak in 1979, when 25 million Americans—14.1 percent of the population— were marijuana users. At the time, many policymakers feared that marijuana use, especially among young people, had gotten out of hand. The National Institute on Drug Abuse explains: "In the 1970s, the baby boom generation was coming of age, and its

a "determination of values." In the case of the Controlled Substances Act, the statute reflects a determination that marijuana has no medical benefits worthy of an exception. . . . Indeed, for purposes of the Controlled Substances Act, marijuana has "no currently accepted medical use" at all. . . .

According to the Cooperative, a drug may not yet have achieved general acceptance as a medical treatment but may nonetheless have medical benefits to a particular patient or class of patients. . . . It is clear from the text of the Act that Congress has made a determination that marijuana has no medical benefits worthy of an exception.

Three justices, however, said that they would not have denied doctors or their patients to raise the defense of medical necessity. Justice John Paul Stevens explained:

Most notably, whether the defense might be available to a seriously ill patient for whom there is no alternative means of avoiding starvation or extraordinary suffering is a difficult issue that is not presented here. . . .

By passing Proposition 215, California voters have decided that seriously ill patients and their primary caregivers should be exempt from prosecution under state laws for cultivating and possessing marijuana if the patient's physician recommends using the drug for treatment.

Note: *Oakland Cannabis* dealt with a marijuana provider's, not a patient's, claim of medical necessity.

drug of choice was marijuana. By 1979, more than 60 percent of 12th-graders had tried marijuana at least once in their lives. From this peak, the percentage of 12th-graders who had ever

## FROM THE BENCH

### *Gonzales v. Raich*, 545 U.S. 1 (2005)

Angel Raich and Diane Monson were medical marijuana patients who lived in California, where state law permitted them to use the drug on a doctor's recommendation. Their use of marijuana, however, still violated the federal CSA. One day, the DEA raided Monson's home and seized her marijuana plants.

Monson filed a lawsuit in federal court to stop the DEA from raiding her home again. Raich joined the suit because she feared that federal agents would someday target her as well. They argued that enforcing the CSA against them overstepped the boundaries of the Commerce Clause (Article I, Section 8 of the U.S. Constitution), which gave Congress the power "[t]o make all Laws which shall be necessary and proper for carrying into Execution" its authority to "regulate Commerce with foreign Nations, and among the several States." In their view, noncommercial cultivation and use of marijuana within the boundaries of California was not "interstate commerce."

The case went to the U.S. Supreme Court, which, in *Gonzales v. Raich*, held that the CSA applied to the noncommercial use of medical marijuana. The vote was 6-to-3. Justice John Paul Stevens, who wrote the majority opinion, noted that Congress, in passing the CSA, stated that its objectives were to conquer drug abuse and to control the legitimate and illegitimate traffic in controlled substances, and that Congress was especially concerned with preventing the diversion of drugs from legitimate to illicit channels.

Stevens concluded that medical marijuana had a "substantial effect" on interstate commerce and therefore justified regulation. He found the facts of this case similar to a 1942 case, *Wickard v. Filburn*, in which the Court upheld federal limits on how much wheat farmers could grow, even when the extra wheat was used by the farmer himself and not put into the stream of commerce. The Court concluded in *Wickard* that intrastate wheat production would undercut the regulation of the interstate market in wheat and thus could be regulated. In the same manner, "diversion of homegrown marijuana tends to frustrate the federal interest in eliminating commercial transactions in the interstate market in their entirety." Stevens said he had "no difficulty concluding that Congress had a rational basis for believing that failure to regulate the intrastate manufacture and possession of marijuana would leave a gaping hole in the CSA."

used marijuana decreased for more than a decade, dropping to a low of 33 percent in 1992."[14] Today, there are 10 million fewer current users than there were 30 years ago, even though

---

Stevens next rejected Raich and Monson's arguments that the CSA did not apply to medical-marijuana patients. First, the fact that they were using marijuana for medical reasons was of no consequence, since the CSA made no exception for such use. Second, although medical marijuana was legal in California, the Supremacy Clause of the Constitution provided that federal law regulating commerce took precedence over conflicting state law. Finally, medical-marijuana users were not "isolated" from the larger marijuana market because it was too easy to cross the line between medical and recreational production and use.

Stevens went on to suggest that the courts were the wrong forum for changing marijuana laws. He said: "But perhaps even more important than these legal avenues is the democratic process, in which the voices of voters allied with these respondents may one day be heard in the halls of Congress."

Justice Sandra Day O'Connor, one of the three dissenters, argued that California's Compassionate Use Act was an example of states acting as "laboratories" for social policy. She wrote: "Today the Court sanctions an application of the federal Controlled Substances Act that extinguishes that experiment, without any proof that the personal cultivation, possession, and use of marijuana for medicinal purposes, if economic activity in the first place, has a substantial effect on interstate commerce." Another dissenter, Justice Clarence Thomas, argued that medical marijuana did not have a "substantial effect" on interstate commerce. If Congress could regulate marijuana that was neither bought nor sold and that did not cross state lines, he warned, then it could regulate virtually anything.

The Supreme Court sent the case back to the lower courts to hear Raich and Monson's remaining arguments. Monson later withdrew from the suit, but Raich continued her efforts to stop the government from enforcing the CSA. Raich argued that she needed to use marijuana to stay alive, and thus had a "medical necessity" defense against criminal charges under the CSA; and also argued that she had a constitutional right to use medical marijuana. In *Raich v. Gonzales*, 500 F.3d 850 (9th Cir. 2007), however, a federal appeals court rejected both arguments.

*Raich* did not invalidate state medical marijuana laws. It did, however, confirm the authority of federal authorities to enforce the CSA against medical-marijuana patients and their caregivers—even in states with medical-marijuana programs.

nation's population has grown, and the percentage of daily users is down by more than half. A Monitoring the Future survey found that teenage marijuana use in the United States fell by 19 percent between 2001 to 2005. That period coincides with the first term of President George W. Bush, whose administration took a hard line against drugs.

Marijuana laws can accomplish other goals besides reducing the number of users. Arrests for possession not only discourage people from using the drug, but also help cut off supply. For example, a prosecutor might offer to dismiss a possession charge if the person charged tells what he or she knows about dealers who are selling the drug, or might offer a small-time dealer a chance to plead guilty to simple possession in exchange for a promise to get out of the drug business. The criminal justice system can also force offenders to deal with their dependence on drugs. An approach that has grown in popularity is so-called "drug courts." Created to deal with low-level drug offenders, these courts offer the opportunity to go into treatment as an alternative to jail. The ONDCP says:

> In recent years, with the introduction of drug courts and similar programs, there has been a shift within the U.S. criminal justice system toward providing treatment rather than incarceration for drug users and nonviolent offenders with addiction problems. Today, in fact, the criminal justice system is the largest source of referral to drug treatment programs.[15]

Some argue that strictly enforcing marijuana laws helps reduce crime in general. When Rudy Giuliani was mayor of New York City, he cracked down on "quality of life" violations—low-level crimes including marijuana possession. This approach was based on the philosophy of "broken windows": tolerating minor crime allows a criminal element to take root in a community, leading to more serious criminal behavior. Aggressively pursuing minor offenders also increases the chances that the police will also catch more dangerous criminals. Giuliani's strategy is widely considered a success—violent crime in the city fell sharply during his administration. Other cities observed what happened in New York, and adopted similar policies.

## Summary

There is no such thing as a "victimless crime" because all behavior, by definition, affects others. The harm attributable to marijuana abuse ranges from lost productivity to drug-related violence by organized criminals. In addition, many people are offended by marijuana users and their lifestyle. Society is justified in making a statement that using marijuana is wrong, and by using the law as a means of doing so. Arresting marijuana users is an appropriate response, especially since small-time users rarely go to jail and few people are in prison for possession alone. Tough law enforcement has prevented marijuana use from becoming uncontrollable. Most Americans still favor marijuana prohibition, and many would consider a decision to liberalize that policy as rewarding those who had broken the law.

# Enforcing Marijuana Prohibition Is Destructive and Wasteful

When the United States took a second look at its marijuana policy in the 1960s, one result was new laws that carried milder penalties for simple possession and use. Nevertheless, a growing number of users find themselves in trouble with the law. In 1972, the year the Shafer Commission called for the elimination of penalties for using marijuana in private, police made almost 300,000 marijuana arrests. That number has steadily risen. In 2000, there were 646,042 arrests for possession alone; in 2007, the total had risen to 872,721. The policy of mass arrests for marijuana violations has many Americans asking whether the punishment fits the crime. Some even wonder whether the "war on marijuana" is worth fighting.

## Marijuana laws are harsher than people realize.

The widely held belief that marijuana use is a minor offense is not always true. "Aggravating factors," such as giving the drug to a minor or possessing it in a "drug free zone," can result in heavier penalties. Some states still treat people who give marijuana to their friends, or ask them to split the cost, as "sellers," who are treated much more harshly. Growing marijuana plants can result in penalties as severe as those for selling the drug. Under federal law, growing just one plant is punishable by up to five years in prison and a $250,000 fine. Journalist Eric Schlosser cites an example of how disproportionate marijuana penalties can be:

> Jim Montgomery, a paraplegic immobilized from the waist down, who smoked marijuana to relieve muscle spasms, was arrested in Sayre, Oklahoma, when sheriffs found two ounces of pot in the pouch on the back of his wheelchair. Montgomery was tried and convicted in 1992, by a jury, for possession of marijuana with intent to distribute, for possession of paraphernalia, for unlawful possession of a weapon during the commission of a crime (two handguns inherited from his father, a police officer), and for maintaining a place resorted to by users of controlled substances. His sentence was life in prison, plus sixteen years.[1]

Even a charge of simple possession can have serious consequences. Peter Brady, a correspondent for *Cannabis Culture*, explains:

> Being arrested for pot involves being detained, interrogated, forced to provide identification, held against one's will. It involves fear of punishment. It involves entering the byzantine labyrinth of the criminal justice system, at the mercy of guards, violent prisoners, bail bondsmen, jurors, judges, and attorneys. It involves expenditure of money.

*(continues on page 72)*

## Major Studies of Marijuana Policy

### The Indian Hemp Drugs Commission Report, 1894

The first extensive marijuana study looked at the use of this drug in British India. It concluded that moderate use of the drug was the rule, moderate users experienced few ill effects, and excessive use was comparatively rare.

### Panama Canal Zone Military Investigations, 1929

A panel of military and civilian experts studied marijuana smoking by servicemen in the Canal Zone. It found no evidence that the marijuana grown and used there was habit-forming and recommended against prohibiting the sale or use of the drug.

### The La Guardia Committee Report, 1944

After conducting a thorough study of the history of marijuana and how it was used in New York City, the committee found that marijuana was not addictive, did not lead to harder drugs, and that its dangers had been exaggerated.

### The Wootton Report, 1968

A panel of leading British drug-abuse experts concluded that marijuana did not have serious physical consequences; did not cause serious dependence or psychosis in normal users; did not lead to heroin addiction; and, compared with alcohol, was less strongly associated with violent crime.

### The Le Dain Report, 1970

A panel of Canadian experts determined that marijuana use did not constitute a serious threat to the public welfare. It recommended giving serious consideration to legalizing the possession and growing of marijuana and the giving away of small amounts of the drug.

### The Shafer Commission Report, 1972

An American panel, which included several elected officials, recommended eliminating penalties for the simple possession and use of marijuana in private. Its recommendation was endorsed by, among other groups, organizations representing the nation's doctors and lawyers.

### Canadian Government Report, 1979

The Canadian government concluded that relaxing marijuana laws would not endanger public health. Like the Shafer Commission, it recommended eliminating the ban on simple possession or use, while continuing to outlaw trafficking.

### National Academy of Sciences Report, 1982

The academy's panel concluded that while marijuana was not harmless, total prohibition of the drug did more harm than good. It recommended repealing federal marijuana laws and allowing states to regulate the drug as they saw fit, including legalizing it along the lines of alcohol.

### California Research Advisory Panel Report, 1989

The panel, appointed by the state legislature, recommended a policy of "regulation and decriminalization" of marijuana, which would include allowing Californians to grow marijuana for personal use.

### The Australian Government Report, 1994

The report found little evidence that the use of small amounts of marijuana caused significant harm and that marijuana use was commonplace despite strict laws against it. It concluded that Australia's existing laws were doing society more harm than good.

### Connecticut Law Revision Commission Report, 1997

The commission found that states that had decriminalized marijuana spent fewer resources on arresting and prosecuting users, yet experienced smaller increases in marijuana use than states that had not. It recommended decriminalizing possession of an ounce or less of marijuana by people 21 or older.

### The Institute of Medicine Study, 1999

The Institute of Medicine, part of the National Academy of Sciences, issued a report dealing with the possible benefits of medical marijuana. The IOM report took a cautious middle course, and its findings have been cited by advocates on both sides of the controversy. It called for higher-quality scientific studies of medical marijuana, including clinical trials aimed at developing a safer alternative to smoking the drug.

### The New Mexico Governor's Drug Policy Report, 2001

An advisory group to the governor recommended decriminalizing the possession of one ounce or less of marijuana by people 18 or older. It argued that decriminalization would allow the criminal justice system to focus on more serious crimes without jeopardizing public safety.

### British Advisory Council on the Misuse of Drugs, 2002

The council concluded that marijuana was less harmful than other substances—including amphetamines, barbiturates, and codeine-like compounds—that

*(continues)*

*(continued)*
Parliament placed within Class B of the Misuse of Drugs Act. It found that grouping marijuana with more harmful Class B drugs could suggest to users that if they had no harmful effects from marijuana, they would likewise suffer no such effects if they used "harder" drugs in that class. It therefore moved marijuana to Class C, a group of less-dangerous illegal drugs.

*(continued from page 69)*

> In some cases, arrest and consequences of arrest are much harsher than the minimum. . . . If convicted of a marijuana crime, a person can lose school funding, child custody, professional credentials, the right to vote, the ability to get a good job.[2]

Critics also contend that the authorities waste resources on catching small-time users, while providing little help to those struggling with drug problems. Between 1981, when the "war on drugs" began in earnest, and 1991, federal spending on law enforcement increased by more than 700 percent. Today, we spend seven times as much on drug interdiction (disruption of supply), enforcement activity, and imprisonment than we spend on treatment. Some question the heavy emphasis on law enforcement. The Connecticut Law Revision Commission observed: "As a means of 'solving' the drug problem, it appears that the state's heavy reliance on the criminal justice system is misplaced. One federal prosecutor in Connecticut observed that 'it is clear that we can't arrest our way out of the drug problem.' "[3]

## Enforcement has little effect on supply or demand.

One objective of marijuana laws is to deter people from using the drug. In 2008, authorities made their ten-millionth marijuana arrest since the Marijuana Tax Act became law. Neither those arrests, nor the expenditure of billions of dollars on enforcement, has had much of an effect on marijuana use. The Justice Policy Institute notes that for decades, the number of marijuana users has fluctuated between four and five percent of Americans. It adds that there is little correlation between arrest rates and marijuana use:

> Starting in 1979, use rates began a precipitous decline—falling 61 percent by 1991, while arrest rates declined by only 24 percent in the same time period. When arrests rose sharply in the 1990s, use for the most part increased or remained the same. From 1991 to 2003, the number of arrests increased by 127 percent, while use rates remained relatively level, climbing only 22 percent.[4]

Eric Schlosser adds: "One of the great ironies of American drug policy is that anti-drug laws over the past century have tended to become most punitive long after the use of a drug has peaked.[5]

Another objective of marijuana laws is to "dry up" the market for the drug and thus discourage people from growing and selling it. By that standard as well, the laws have not succeeded. According to the National Office of Drug Control Policy, the price of marijuana remained relatively stable during the 1990s, but the total seizures by federal authorities rose by more than 400 percent, and more potent strains of the drug appeared on the market. The Sentencing Project reports that during roughly that same period, the inflation-adjusted price of marijuana fell by 16 percent, while its potency increased by 53 percent. All of this happened while the number of marijuana arrests steadily climbed.

Still another way of measuring the impact of marijuana laws is to compare states with tough laws against those with more lenient ones. The Connecticut Law Revision Commission made such a comparison. It found that the cost of arresting and prosecuting marijuana offenders was significantly lower in states

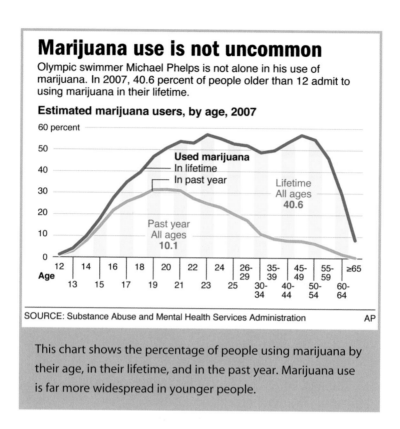

**Marijuana use is not uncommon**

Olympic swimmer Michael Phelps is not alone in his use of marijuana. In 2007, 40.6 percent of people older than 12 admit to using marijuana in their lifetime.

**Estimated marijuana users, by age, 2007**

SOURCE: Substance Abuse and Mental Health Services Administration    AP

This chart shows the percentage of people using marijuana by their age, in their lifetime, and in the past year. Marijuana use is far more widespread in younger people.

that had done away with criminal penalties for possessing small amounts; that there was a greater increase in marijuana use in states that continued to treat possession as a crime than in states that had downgraded it to a civil offense; and that easing the penalties for marijuana did not lead to a substantial increase in the use of either alcohol or hard drugs.

## Marijuana laws divert resources from more serious problems.

Even assuming that drug prohibition reduces demand, law enforcement agencies are concentrating on the wrong drug. The Sentencing Project points out that marijuana accounts for nearly half of all drug-related arrests, and that marijuana arrests actually increased by 113 percent between 1990 and 2002 while overall arrests in the nation decreased by 3 percent. In fact, more Americans are arrested for marijuana than for heroin and cocaine combined, although heroin and cocaine are far more dangerous. While no one knows exactly how much money is spent on enforcing marijuana laws, Jeffrey Miron, an economist, estimated that state and local governments spend more than $5 billion a year and that the federal government spends an additional $2.6 billion a year on drug interdiction alone.

Supporters insist that a more liberal marijuana policy would not leave society defenseless. To begin with, the government would still be able to pursue traffickers. If marijuana were legalized, unauthorized sales would be treated in much the same way as running an unlicensed nightclub or selling bootleg cigarettes. If the drug were decriminalized, existing laws against trafficking would likely stay on the books, and traffickers would still face harsh penalties. In addition, the law would continue to deal firmly with abuse of the drug. Public use would probably be illegal, just as public drinking is in much of the country. Furthermore, irresponsible marijuana use would result in serious legal consequences. The Shafer Commission recommended:

> First, the "drunk and disorderly" statutes presently in force in the states are useful tools for maintaining public order. We would suggest similar statutes in the case of marijuana, punishing offenders by up to 60 days in jail, a fine of $100, or both....
>
> The second aspect of irresponsible behavior is the operation of automobiles, other vehicles, or any potentially dangerous instrument while under the influence of marijuana.... In addition to penalizing a person who "drives under the influence" as a serious misdemeanant, we would impose absolute civil liability on anyone who harms the person or property of another while under the influence of marijuana.

Finally, no one should be able to limit his criminal accountability by alleging that he was under the influence of marijuana at the time of the crime.[6]

Those who favor relaxing the marijuana laws also contend that tough laws, combined with widespread demand for the

## FROM THE BENCH

### Conant v. Walters, 309 F.3d 629 (9th Cir. 2002)

After California legalized medical marijuana in 1996, federal authorities made it clear that the use of marijuana for any purpose, even treating a medical condition, was still illegal. The federal government even warned doctors that if they prescribed marijuana or recommended that their patients use it, they could lose the ability to write prescriptions for federally controlled drugs.

A number of doctors went to court to stop the government from taking action against them. The doctors argued that regardless of marijuana's legal status, they had the same First Amendment right of free speech as other Americans. Their lawsuit went to the United States Court of Appeals for the Ninth Circuit, which, in *Conant v. Walters*, concluded that the government's actions violated the doctors' First Amendment rights. Here are excerpts from Chief Judge Mary Schroeder's opinion:

> The government policy does, however, strike at core First Amendment interests of doctors and patients. An integral component of the practice of medicine is the communication between a doctor and a patient. Physicians must be able to speak frankly and openly to patients. . . .
>
> Being a member of a regulated profession does not . . . result in a surrender of First Amendment rights. . . . To the contrary, professional speech may be entitled to "the strongest protection our Constitution has to offer."
>
> The government's policy in this case seeks to punish physicians on the basis of the content of doctor-patient communications. Only doctor-patient communications that include discussions of the medical use of marijuana trigger the policy. Moreover, the policy does not merely prohibit the discussion of marijuana; it condemns expression of a particular viewpoint, i.e., that medical marijuana would likely help a specific patient.

drug, have created a vast and lucrative black market that organized criminals are eager to serve. The editors of *Consumer Reports* explain: "The very severity of law enforcement tends to increase the price of drugs on the illicit market and the profits to be made there from. The lure of profits and the risks of the traffic simply challenge the ingenuity of the underworld peddlers

Such condemnation of particular views is especially troubling in the First Amendment context.

Judge Alex Kozinski wrote a concurring opinion, in which he explained in greater detail his belief that the federal policy was unconstitutional and did more harm than good:

> To those unfamiliar with the issue, it may seem faddish or foolish for a doctor to recommend a drug that the federal government finds has "no currently accepted medical use in the United States"... But the record in this case, as well as the public record, reflect a legitimate and growing division of informed opinion on this issue...
>
> In the absence of sound medical advice, many patients desperate for relief from debilitating pain or nausea would self-medicate, and wind up administering the wrong dose or frequency, or use the drug where a physician would advise against it. Whatever else the parties may disagree about, they agree that marijuana is a powerful and complex drug, the kind of drug patients should not use without careful professional supervision...
>
> [M]uch as the federal government may prefer that California keep medical marijuana illegal, it cannot force the state to do so. Yet, the effect of the federal government's policy is precisely that... In effect, the federal government is forcing the state to keep medical marijuana illegal...
>
> The doctor-patient relationship is an area that falls squarely within the states' traditional police powers. The federal government may not force the states to regulate that relationship to advance federal policy...

In October 2003, the U.S. Supreme Court refused to hear the government's appeal, thus letting the Ninth Circuit's opinion stand.

to find new channels of distribution and new customers, so that profits can be maintained."[7] Black-market profits are irresistible to the underworld. During Prohibition, the newly illegal liquor trade attracted gangsters such as Al Capone; today, much of America's demand for marijuana is being met by organized criminals.

## Enforcement is arbitrary and endangers civil liberties, particularly of minorities.

According to the 2002 National Survey on Drug Use and Health, 14 percent of regular marijuana users are African Americans. The Sentencing Project, however, found that African Americans account for 30 percent of those arrested for marijuana violations. To put it another way, whites are more likely to be "let off." Activist Jon Gettman observed:

> Police exercise a great deal of discretion in their professional decision making. Respect for this discretion is one of the most important professional values in the field of law enforcement. Like other so-called "victimless crimes," drug possession offenses provide some of the greatest latitude for police discretion. In many instances confiscation and a warning are justified alternatives to arrest, especially when marijuana is involved.[8]

The fact that only a small fraction of marijuana users are arrested adds to the perception that the police arbitrarily enforce the law. The probability that a user will be arrested in a given year has been estimated at three percent. Many people use marijuana dozens, even hundreds, of times a year, which means that the chance of their being arrested for a given violation is minuscule. Laws that are so widely broken invite arbitrary, even abusive, enforcement—a problem suggested by the difference in white and African-American arrest rates. Enforcing the law selectively, especially with the intention of making an example of somebody, creates a sense of injustice and may cause loss of respect for the law.

Drug prohibition also has a corrosive effect on civil liberties. According to the Sentencing Project: "Since relatively few drug crimes are reported to police, tactics used by law enforcement have increasingly included surveillance and undercover operations."[9] These operations often take place in inner cities, reinforcing the perception that authorities target minority groups for drug-law violations. In pursuing their goal of a drug-free America, authorities sometimes operate on the outer fringes of the Bill of Rights: sealing off public housing projects for house-to-house inspections; searching cars without a warrant; using anonymous tips and drug-courier profiles as the basis for searches; and seizing legal fees from lawyers representing people charged with drug crimes. Drug prohibition even extends to peoples' homes, something many Americans believe is contrary to the time-honored belief that "a man's home is his castle." In fact, drug prohibition is even more intrusive than national alcohol prohibition between 1920 and 1933. During that era, only a handful of states made it illegal for adults to possess alcohol for their personal use.

## Marijuana prohibition encourages dangerous drug taking.

Marijuana prohibition forces users to buy their marijuana on the black market, where they are more likely to come in contact with both criminals and hard drugs. As the Canadian Senate committee found, "the sociological conditions under which users can obtain cannabis are such that they are in contact with an environment that is at least marginal if not criminal. Dealers are often the same people who sell heroin, crack, amphetamines, cocaine and Ecstasy."[10] Marijuana prohibition can also turn otherwise law-abiding citizens into outlaws. The Consumers Union observed: "Engaging in criminal behavior has a subtle but significant effect on the self-image of individuals. Because they are criminals under the law, they begin to think of themselves as criminals. Lacking respect for the marijuana laws, they may lose respect for other laws as well."[11]

Paradoxically, marijuana prohibition also may contribute to abuse of the drug. A National Academy of Sciences panel found that marijuana's status as "forbidden fruit" makes it more likely that young people will be introduced to it by their heavy-drug-using friends rather than family members who are more likely to use it in moderation. Prohibition also interferes with efforts

## "Reefer Madness"? The Case of Mark Young

Opponents of marijuana prohibition often cite stories of Americans who receive heavy sentences for relatively minor offenses. In 1994, journalist Eric Schlosser recounted the case of Mark Young, one such victim of modern-day "Reefer Madness." Young was sentenced to life in prison without the possibility of parole by a federal judge in Indiana for having entered into an agreement with two other men to find buyers for the marijuana they were growing on a nearby farm. According to Schlosser, Young's punishment did not fit the crime: "He had never before been charged with drug trafficking. He had no history of violent crime. . . . he never distributed the drugs; he simply introduced two people hoping to sell a large amount of marijuana to three people wishing to buy it. . . . He was convicted solely on the testimony of co-conspirators who were now cooperating with the government."

Schlosser explains that federal drug laws led to Young's heavy sentence. When he got involved in the marijuana transaction, Young was well into his thirties. As a young man, he accumulated two felony convictions for drugs. One, at the age of 22, was for attempting to pass a fraudulent prescription. The second, at the age of 26, was for possessing a few amphetamines and Quaaludes. Each of these convictions resulted in a suspended sentence, probation, and a $1 fine. Under federal law, however, those offenses combined with marijuana cases counted as prior felony convictions and classified him as a "three strikes" career drug offender. Furthermore, federal drug laws are so sweeping that Young was charged not only for his role in distributing 700 pounds of marijuana but also to curb excessive use. The Shafer Commission found that the possibility of criminal prosecution discourages people who have marijuana-related health problems from seeking help and makes it difficult to provide honest information about the drug. The Canadian Senate observed that government officials often regard any use of an illegal drug as "abuse" and therefore fail to make a distinction between low-risk and high-risk use of that drug.

Marijuana prohibition might even contribute to heavy drinking. Some contend that alcohol and marijuana are substitutes for

for conspiring to grow all 12,500 plants that were turned into the marijuana that was eventually sold.

The National Office of Drug Control Policy contends that Schlosser's account leaves out several important facts about the case.* To begin with, that case did not involve a casual drug transaction. Young brokered a deal between a group of growers who wanted to sell large quantities of marijuana and a group of traffickers who wanted to buy it. That transaction involved 700 pounds of marijuana, worth about $700,000, and Young took at least $60,000 in commissions before police discovered the scheme, broke up the ring, and arrested its members. As a result, Young was charged with a serious offense—namely, conspiracy to manufacture more than 1,000 marijuana plants. Even though Young's two prior convictions qualified him for a long prison term, the U.S. Attorney's Office offered him a plea bargain. If he agreed to testify against his co-conspirators, the government would ask for a greatly reduced sentence. Young not only refused to cooperate, but also threatened to have his former partners killed, along with their families.

The ONDCP adds that Schlosser's story leaves out what happened after Young was sentenced. A federal appeals court reduced the sentence to 12½ years. Young served his time and got out on supervised release, only to be sent back for another six months because he failed several drug tests. After serving those six months, he was sent back to prison for nine more months for failing one drug test and not showing up for another.

* Office of National Drug Control Policy, *Who's Really in Prison for Marijuana?* Washington, D.C., 2005.

one another, and, therefore, tough enforcement against marijuana leads to greater use of alcohol. There is support for that
argument. When alcohol was prohibited in the United States,
bars in some cities gave way to "tea pads" where marijuana was
smoked; when marijuana experienced an upsurge of popularity
in the 1960s, alcohol consumption fell in some communities,
especially college towns. At the time, the editors of *Consumer
Reports* argued: "A knowledgeable society, noting a few years
ago that some of its members were switching from alcohol to
a less harmful intoxicant, marijuana, might have encouraged
that trend. At the very least, society could have stressed the
advantages of cutting down alcohol consumption if you smoke
marijuana."[12]

## Summary

Nearly 40 years ago, the Shafer Commission recommended the
elimination of criminal penalties for marijuana use in private.
Policymakers ignored that recommendation, and today authorities arrest hundreds of thousands of Americans every year in an
effort to eliminate marijuana use. Many of those arrested go to
jail or suffer other serious consequences. Some are sentenced
to long prison terms. Members of minority groups are arrested
more frequently for marijuana offenses than whites, raising serious questions of fairness. Despite the growing number of arrests,
millions of Americans use marijuana, and a black market in the
drug continues to thrive. Some believe that marijuana prohibition does more harm than good by encouraging would-be users
to turn to more dangerous drugs.

# Relaxing Marijuana Laws Would Cause Serious Problems

In 1994, a panel of the New York City Bar recommended an end to drug prohibition. The dissenting members of that panel argued that the majority had ignored the social harm that would result from legalization:

> In characterizing drug abuse as a "right of individuals" the Report ignores its social costs, which include physical damage to babies born of drug using mothers; abuse and/or neglect by users of parents, offspring, friends and relatives; death by overdose; teen suicides; homelessness; drug-induced altered states of consciousness producing violence, particularly from the use of cocaine and crack; loss of productivity of drug-using workers; waste of educational resources used in attempts to teach drug-abusing students; the ripple effect on the economy

from the presence of large numbers of incapacitated or impaired individuals; and the enormous cost of drug treatment programs.[1]

## Relaxing marijuana laws would lead to more use.

If marijuana laws were relaxed, the number of users and the amount of marijuana used would increase. John Walters, the former director of the White House Office of National Drug Control Policy, said:

> Some people believe drugs such as cocaine and heroin should be legal, sold by the government and regulated like alcohol. Our experience with alcohol (some 127 million regular drinkers as compared to fewer than 20 million drug users) suggests this would be a huge mistake. It is hard to imagine an aspect of American life that would be enriched by millions of new cocaine, heroin or marijuana users.[2]

The Shafer Commission observed that legalization "could be expected to bring about an increase in users, with some percentage of them becoming heavy users. It is the availability of the drug, coupled with a governmental policy of approval or neutrality, that could escalate this group into a public health and welfare concern. While this is speculative, it is a concern which cannot be dismissed."[3] The commission also worried that legalization might create a population of hard-core users like that found in some countries such as Jamaica, and that those users would become a serious public health concern.

Legalizing marijuana would increase consumption. First of all, with little or no black-market premium, the drug probably would become cheaper, perhaps much cheaper. In 1994, Dale Gieringer of the National Organization for the Reform of Marijuana Laws speculated that a "joint" that then sold for $6 would cost less than six cents, making it cheap compared with other intoxicants. Prices that low could result in a population of heavy users, who would recruit others into a drug-oriented way of life. Legal marijuana also would also be more widely available, especially to those who currently have no connection to a black-market supplier; and, if marijuana were legal, existing users might turn to more potent forms of it. Some would-be users might interpret a shift in policy away from prohibition as an endorsement of the drug, especially if the government started urging people to "be careful" with it.

Removing the risk of arrest gives people one more reason to try the drug. In support of that argument, the Drug Enforcement Administration cites R.E. Peterson's study of the relationship between enforcement and drug use since 1960:

> The first period, from 1960 to 1980, was an era of permissive drug laws. During this era, drug incarceration rates fell almost 80 percent. Drug use among teens, meanwhile, climbed by more than 500 percent. The second period, from 1980 to 1995, was an era of stronger drug laws. During this era, drug use by teens dropped by more than a third.[4]

Some argue that if the authorities had not arrested millions of people for using marijuana, today's usage levels might be even higher than the record-high levels of the late 1970s.

## Relaxing the laws would make marijuana even more available to young people.

Even though tobacco and alcohol have been legal for most of the past 400 years, Americans still disagree as to how they should be regulated. Even more serious concerns would arise if marijuana were legalized. When and where could it be sold? Some supporters of legalization want to extend the alcohol-control model to marijuana; in fact, legislation that would legalize marijuana in California proposed doing just that. Many people, however, believe that our laws already make it too easy to buy liquor. In much of the country, beer and wine can be sold in supermarkets

## The Case for Not Legalizing Drugs

In 1994, a special committee of the New York City Bar Association wrote a paper titled *A Wiser Course: Ending Drug Prohibition.** The committee's recommendation, that drug prohibition be ended, was not unanimous. Several members issued a dissenting opinion in which they detailed the damaging consequences of legalization. Here some are excerpts from their dissent:

> Our disagreement is based upon our concern that the legal sale of drugs would increase substantially the number of persons who use and/or become addicted to drugs, causing harm not only to themselves but to society. Such harm would, in our view, outweigh the benefits of eliminating drug prohibition.

### 1. Legalizing Drugs Would Reduce Their Cost to the Public, Thereby Increasing Demand, Use and Addiction

The theory of drug legalization is that it would take the profit motive out of illegal drug dealing, eliminating the evils of drug prohibition. In order to accomplish this result drugs would have to be sold at prices lower than their present illicit levels. Many commentators have reached the conclusion that lower prices would increase the demand for drugs....

### 2. The Report Fails to Provide a Concrete Proposal

Certainly, if we accept the proposition advanced by many commentators that the legal sale of drugs, at lower prices than the prices of illegal drugs, would greatly widen demand, we should reject the proposal that such harmful substances as those mentioned above be legally sold or that any drugs be sold to minors. On the other hand, prohibition of sale of those substances, or of drugs generally to minors, would give illegal drug traffickers a continuing opportunity to exploit these markets, and thus by definition the proposal would not end the evils of drug prohibition....

### 3. The Report Does Not Set Forth Any Convincing Basis for Its Conclusion That "'Use in Continued Moderation' Would Be The Much More Likely Result of Decriminalization"

and convenience stores, and sales are allowed seven days of the week and most hours of the day. Similar regulations might make it too easy to buy marijuana before school opens and

None of the evidence cited in the Report refutes the strong likelihood that reducing prices and facilitating access would significantly increase demand for drugs. . . .

The results of Prohibition suggest a correlation between prohibition and use. Alcohol use declined at the outset of Prohibition and then increased to only 60% to 70% of pre-Prohibition levels. Immediately after Repeal, alcohol use remained the same, but it increased to pre-Prohibition levels during the next decade. . . .

**4. The Report is Mistaken in Characterizing Drug Abuse as an Individual "Right" Rather Than as a Social Evil**

In characterizing drug abuse as a 'right of individuals' the Report ignores its social costs, which include physical damage to babies born of drug using mothers; abuse and/or neglect by users of parents, offspring, friends and relatives; death by overdose; teen suicides; homelessness; drug-induced altered states of consciousness producing violence, particularly from the use of cocaine and crack; loss of productivity of drug-using workers; waste of educational resources used in attempts to teach drug-abusing students; the ripple effect on the economy from the presence of large numbers of inca-pacitated or impaired individuals; and the enormous cost of drug treatment programs. . . .

**5. The Report Should Stress the Need to Reduce Demand for Drugs Without Endorsing Legalization**

The Report is enormously thoughtful and comprehensive and deserves the most serious study. It describes accurately and completely the importance and effectiveness of harm reduction and drug treatment programs. For the reasons stated above, however, the Report should not recommend ending drug prohi-bition. Because of the risk of catastrophic social harm from legalization, many of the most thoughtful recent works on this topic do not recommend this approach.

* Association of the Bar of the City of New York. *A Wiser Course: Ending Drug Prohibition.* New York, 1994, http://www.druglibrary.org/schaffer/library/studies/nylawyer/nylawyer.htm.

during working hours. Because marijuana impairs one's ability to drive, especially when used in combination with alcohol, there would be strong sentiment for outlawing its use, let alone its sale, in bars and other public establishments. Citizens also would demand tough restrictions aimed at keeping the drug from being sold too close to where young people gather. There might also be demands for a potency limit. The Canadian Senate committee recommended a very high limit of 13 percent THC, but lawmakers could insist on a much lower limit as a means of discouraging heavy use. Limiting potency, however, might not be practical. As the Shafer Commission observed: "This is not an easy undertaking. Especially when cannabis is so easily grown and a black market is so easily created, we are dubious about the success of a regulatory scheme distributing only a product with low THC content."[5]

The alcohol and tobacco industries have been accused of irresponsibly marketing their products. If marijuana were legal, it might be marketed in the same fashion. Advertising is a particular concern. Because advertising is "commercial speech" protected by the First Amendment, the government has limited power to control the advertising of legal products. Many Americans are offended by advertisements for beer, gambling casinos, and prescription drugs designed to improve men's sexual performance. They would object even more strongly to advertisements for marijuana. There is also the danger that the legal-marijuana industry would promote the product to underage customers or people likely to abuse it. Mark Kleiman, a professor at the University of California, Los Angeles, warned: "Any sort of flat-out legalization would risk a large increase in the number of very heavy users. A legal cannabis industry, like the legal alcohol industry, would derive more than half its revenue from people with diagnosable substance abuse disorders. Telling marketers they can get rich by creating disease is dangerous."[6]

The most intense debate likely would involve the minimum age for buying marijuana. The Canadian Senate committee proposed a minimum age of 16, three years before most Canadians can legally smoke or drink. Even many supporters of legalization are hesitant to allow people that young to buy the drug. Legislation that would legalize the drug in California made the minimum age 21, the same as it is for alcohol. A minimum age of 21, however, would mean that most marijuana use would still be illegal because a substantial percentage of marijuana users are in their teens: Two-thirds of Americans first try the drug before the age of 18. As we know from our experience with alcohol, people younger than 21 can easily get it. The 2008 Monitoring the Future study found that 29 percent of tenth-graders and 43 percent of twelfth-graders were "current users" of alcohol, meaning that they had consumed it during the past month. What the Shafer Commission said nearly 40 years ago is still true today: "[T]he lack of success with alcohol and tobacco discourages an assumption that the regulation of supply would minimize use by the younger generation."[7] Alaska's experience provides some insight. In 1975, that state's highest court effectively made it legal for adults to use marijuana at home. According to the DEA, many young Alaskans viewed the decision as a signal to begin using marijuana—even though it applied only to those 19 and older. In 1988, a University of Alaska study found that the state's 12- to 17-year-olds were using marijuana at more than twice the national average for their age group.

Decriminalizing marijuana also raises serious questions. First of all, it is logically inconsistent to tolerate possession and use of marijuana and, at the same time, threaten those who grow or sell it with heavy criminal penalties. Under decriminalization, users either have to grow their own marijuana, an activity that is illegal under federal law, or buy marijuana from a black-market supplier. The government also might be accused of sending a mixed message if it encourages responsible use of a product for which there is no legal market. The Canadian Senate committee, which endorsed legalization, was highly critical of decriminalization. It said:

Some say that decriminalization is a step in the right direction, one that gives society time to become accustomed to cannabis, to convince opponents that chaos will not result, to adopt effective preventive measures. We believe however that this approach is in fact the worst case scenario, depriving the State of a necessary regulatory tool for dealing with the entire production, distribution, and consumption network, and delivering hypocritical messages at the same time.[8]

## QUOTABLE

## Asa Hutchinson, Director of the DEA

In November 2001, Asa Hutchinson, the director of the Drug Enforcement Administration, traveled to Yale Law School to debate the war on drugs with Gary Johnson, the governor of New Mexico, who favored legalization. Here are excerpts from Hutchinson's opening statement:

If we as a nation want to discourage drug use that harms not just individuals, but society as a whole, how do we do it? Well, I believe that we do it through the law—by the law saying it is wrong because it is harmful. Our laws reflect the values of society. The law is the master teacher and guides each generation as to what is acceptable conduct. Our laws have to be enforced....

The legalizers present three basic arguments to support their cause:

1. Individual freedom demands it.

2. The drug war has been a failure.

3. Legalization would reduce the cost of enforcement and incarceration.

First of all, in terms of freedom. How many of you believe in seat belt laws? (show of hands). It looks [to be] about the same number that support marijuana legalization. Well, if you support seat belt laws, drug laws should not be any problem.... I would argue that the state should protect not just

## Legalization will not eliminate the black market.

One highly contentious issue in the debate over legalization is how heavily legal marijuana should be taxed. The federal government and the states impose "sin" taxes on alcohol and tobacco. One purpose of these taxes is to raise revenue. A related purpose is to cover the "external costs" of using these products, such as higher health care costs generated by excessive users. At the same time, "sin taxes" also aim to discourage consumption. Thus if the tax on legal marijuana is too low,

---

individual freedom, but the collective freedom. Drug use harms the family and the community, as well as the individual.

But . . . it also endangers democracy. The essence of our democracy is that freedom is maintained by individual participation, individual sacrifice, and common values. The drug culture erodes and destroys everything that is necessary for democracy to work. When someone is overtaken by drugs, he is not thinking about what he can do for others, for the community, for the family, for our common values. He is simply trying to get the next fix on drugs. We give up freedom when we addict ourselves to drugs. . . .

Secondly, they say we're losing the war on drugs. . . .

Drug use over the last 20 years has been reduced by half. Cocaine use is down by 75 percent in the last 15 years. Those are just statistics, but perhaps it's one of your family members that is part of those victories. We should not judge this social problem differently than other social problems. We are making a difference in this effort.

The third argument that is presented is that legalization would put the cartels and drug dealers out of business. Nonsense. . . . There's always going to be the black market, and there's always going to be criminal organizations looking to profit off others' misery.

Source: Asa Hutchinson, Opening Statement, Yale University Law School Debate with New Mexico Governor Gary Johnson, "The Past, Present, & Future of the War on Drugs," November 15, 2001, New Haven, Conn., http://www.usdoj.gov/dea/speeches/s111501.html.

people would be more likely to abuse it and young people would be better able to afford it. Mindful of that, the sponsor of legislation that would legalize marijuana in California proposed a tax of $50 an ounce.

Taxes are one factor that keep black-market sellers in business. Meredith Lintott, a district attorney in California, said that large-scale marijuana growers, who account for most of the marijuana under cultivation, would simply refuse to file

## THE LETTER OF THE LAW

### International Conventions Against Recreational Drug Use

One argument that has been raised against liberalizing marijuana laws is that it would violate our obligations under international drug-control treaties. For a century, the United States has worked with other countries to curb trafficking in narcotic drugs such as opium. America's interest in international anti-drug efforts dates back to the Spanish-American War of 1898, when a government commission headed by Charles Brent, the Episcopal bishop of the Philippines, studied the drug problem in that country. Brent's commission recommended that narcotics be subject to international control.

In 1906, President Theodore Roosevelt, at Brent's request, convened an international opium conference. Negotiations ultimately resulted in The Hague Convention of 1912, which was aimed primarily at solving the opium problems of China and other Asian countries. The Hague Convention led Congress to pass the Harrison Narcotics Act, which, supporters argued, was needed to bring the United States into compliance with that treaty.

Those early efforts at curbing the opium trade have evolved into several modern-day international conventions—the equivalent of treaties—that commit the international community to eliminate recreational use of a variety of drugs. International conventions rely on criminal laws as the primary means of suppressing illicit drug use. Since 1925, the list of banned drugs has included marijuana.

Currently, three treaties regulate drug use:

- **The Single Convention on Narcotic Drugs** (1961), which created an infrastructure for international drug control. It dictated which tax returns if the drug is legalized. High taxes at the retail level would encourage a black market in untaxed legal marijuana. Such a market exists in cigarettes, the taxes on which vary from state to state. Organized criminals buy cigarettes in low-tax states or on Indian reservations and smuggle them into high-tax states. Similarly, most states operate lotteries, but illegal bookmakers continue to operate because they can offer higher payoffs since they avoid paying taxes.

substances should be controlled, how to add new drugs to the list of banned substances, and what role the United Nations should play in international drug control. The convention also set an ambitious goal of eliminating opium consumption within 15 years and marijuana and cocaine consumption within 25 years.

- **The Convention on Psychotropic Substances** (1971), which was created to respond to the growing variety of drugs that emerged in the 1960s, such as LSD, stimulants, and amphetamines.

- **The Convention Against Illicit Traffic in Narcotic Drugs and Psychotropic Substances** (1988), which deals with questions directly related to drug trafficking, such as how to control precursors (substances that are not dangerous themselves but are used in the production of illicit drugs) and how to combat money laundering.

These conventions reflect the international community's expectation that criminal punishment can bring about a drug-free world or, at least, significantly lower levels of illegal drug production and consumption.

Supporters of prohibition believe that anti-drug conventions are essential to promoting the health and welfare of people throughout the world, and reflect the widely held belief that substance abuse is immoral.

Opponents contend that the conventions discriminate in favor of substances produced by pharmaceutical companies and against those that occur in nature. They also argue that drafters of these treaties knew little about marijuana when they added it to the list of controlled drugs, and that their decision to add it was based on prejudice and emotion.

If marijuana is legalized, drug cartels would not go out of existence, but instead they would turn to other markets, such as hard drugs that would remain illegal. Asa Hutchinson, the former director of the DEA, warned: "If you legalize marijuana, the dealers still have cocaine, methamphetamine, heroin, Ecstasy, and all the other abused drugs. Even if you broaden it, and legalize heroin or cocaine, you've still got methamphetamine and Ecstasy. And if you legalize everything, the dealers will offer a better, cheaper high."[9] Unless legalization were to create a totally free market for marijuana, black-market sellers would exist to avoid licensing requirements for sellers, potency limitations, and especially, minimum age restrictions. The DEA warns that since young people are often the primary target of pushers, many of the criminal organizations that now profit from illegal drugs would continue to market the drug to them.

## Legalizing marijuana will have damaging consequences.

Although we have little experience with outright legalization, California's experience with medical marijuana is cause for concern:

> Marijuana plantations in remote forests cause severe environmental damage. Indoor grow houses in some towns put rentals beyond the reach of students and young families. Rural counties with declining economies cannot attract new businesses because the available work force is caught up in the pot industry. Authorities link the drug to violent crime in otherwise quiet small towns.[10]

Even in the Netherlands, there has been a backlash against that country's policy of official tolerance. About 70 percent of Dutch towns now ban marijuana in coffeehouses; and the government announced its intention to reduce the number of such establishments, especially those near schools and in cities close to international borders that have attracted "drug tourists."

If marijuana is legalized, the result would be a large and profitable marijuana industry, with strong political influence like that of the liquor, tobacco, and legalized gambling industries. Marijuana growers and sellers would resist legislative efforts to re-impose prohibition because that would put them out of business. As the Shafer Commission observed: "It is always extremely difficult to transform a previously acceptable behavior into a disapproved behavior."[11] Our experience with smoking demonstrates how hard it is to change behavior with respect to drug use. Since the 1960s, the medical community has warned of the dangers of smoking, and lawmakers have imposed ever-stricter regulations. Nevertheless, tens of millions of Americans still smoke and smoking remains a serious public health problem. Furthermore, legalizing marijuana could result in health problems on a par with those related to smoking. If future studies prove that marijuana causes cancer or some other disease, growers and sellers of the drug could find themselves in court. Even the government itself might be sued on the theory that imposing quality-control standards for marijuana amounted to a guarantee that the drug was safe.

## Summary

Legalizing marijuana, or even decriminalizing it, could lead to wider use of the drug and more serious problems with dependence. There is evidence that drug prohibition in general, and marijuana prohibition in particular, has reduced the number of users. Since legalization would not mean the end of regulation, society would continue to have problems with the drug—especially keeping it away from young people, who already are the most likely to use it. Nor would legalization eliminate organized crime or the black market. Decriminalization would likewise raise serious questions because the marijuana industry would remain outside the law, unregulated and untaxed. Liberalizing marijuana laws could have serious adverse consequences, and might be difficult to reverse because of the political influence of the legal marijuana industry.

# Regulating Marijuana Is Wiser than Prohibiting It

According to the editors of *Consumer Reports,* when Congress was considering the Marijuana Tax Act in 1937, an editorial in the *Journal of the American Medical Association* warned that marijuana prohibition would be a failure:

> After more than twenty years of federal effort and the expenditure of millions of dollars, the opium and cocaine habits are still widespread. The best efforts of an efficient bureau of narcotics, supplemented by the efforts of an equally efficient bureau of customs, have failed to stop the unlawful flow of opium and coca leaves and their compounds and derivatives, on which the continuance and spread of narcotic addiction depends. . . . What reason is there, then, for believing that any better results can be obtained by direct federal

efforts to suppress a habit arising out of the misuse of such a drug as cannabis? Certainly it is almost as easy to smuggle into the country and to distribute as are opium and coca leaves. Moreover it can be cultivated in many parts of the United States and grows wild in field and forest and along the highways in many places.[1]

The *JAMA* article proved prophetic. More Americans than ever—100 million in all—have tried the drug at least once, and marijuana prohibition has led many to disrespect the law and show contempt for those who enforce it.

## Legal marijuana would be safer.

When a product is illegal, unscrupulous sellers of black-market goods can take advantage of the lack of legal controls. The editors of *Consumer Reports* observed that this happened after alcohol was prohibited, sometimes with tragic results:

> Instead of consuming alcoholic beverages manufactured under the safeguards of state and federal standards ... people now drank "rotgut," some of it adulterated, some of it contaminated. The use of methyl alcohol, a poison, because ethyl alcohol was unavailable or too costly, led to blindness and death; "ginger jake," an adulterant found in bootleg beverages, produced paralysis and death.[2]

This is also true under marijuana prohibition. Poisonous substances and hard drugs have been found in marijuana. A user who gets sick from these substances has no legal recourse because pure-food-and-drug and consumer-protection laws do not apply to illegal substances.

If the drug were legal, a person who bought tainted marijuana could demand a refund or even sue the seller for damages. Legalized marijuana would be subject to other health and safety regulations. Growers would be required to comply with environmental and labor standards, and farms and factories would be subject to inspection. If marijuana has been tampered with, government agencies could order it taken off the market. False advertising and price fixing would be illegal, and suppliers could go to court rather than resort to force to collect debts and settle business disputes. People with criminal records or ties to organized crime would be excluded from the industry.

Furthermore, legalization could curb the use of harder drugs. Marijuana prohibition forces many buyers to buy from

## The Canadian Senate Committee's Legalization Proposal

In 2002, a committee of the Canadian Senate issued a report that, among other things, recommended that Canada legalize marijuana along the lines of alcohol. Specifics of the proposal include:

A. The general aims are: to reduce the harmful effects of criminalizing marijuana; to allow Canadians over 16 to buy marijuana at licensed outlets; and to recognize that marijuana is a mood-altering drug that may endanger one's health, and thus regulate it to prevent at-risk and excessive use.

B. The holder of a distributor's license must be a Canadian resident and may not have a criminal record. A distributor must buy marijuana only from licensed producers, may not advertise marijuana or openly display it, and may not sell to anybody under 16.

C. The holder of a producer's license must be a Canadian resident, may not have a criminal record, and must not be affiliated with the tobacco industry. A producer may grow no more than the amount allowed by the license, may sell only to licensed distributors, may not sell marijuana with a THC content higher than 13 percent, may not advertise marijuana, must follow all rules black-market sources, who might be connected to organized crime or dealing in hard drugs as well. The editors of *Consumer Reports* argued that a legal distribution system

> will have notable advantages for both users and nonusers over the present black market. In particular it would separate the channels of marijuana distribution from heroin channels and from the channels of distribution of other illicit drugs—and will thereby limit the exposure of marijuana smokers to other illicit drugs.[3]

relating to security and record-keeping, and must submit to government inspections.

D. An individual may grow enough marijuana for personal use, but may not advertise, sell, or trade it.

E. Marijuana may not be used in public.

F. International trade in marijuana, other than that permitted by law, is considered trafficking.

G. A National Cannabis Board will be established to regulate the industry and to collect taxes, which will be used to fight trafficking, prevent at-risk use, and fund treatment for excessive users. Local government will continue to develop prevention efforts focused on at-risk use as well as support and treatment programs aimed at excessive use. Additional funds and personnel will be made available to combat smuggling and cross-border trafficking.

The Senate's recommendations never became law. After the Senate committee released its report, the Liberal Party government offered a decriminalization bill, but it failed to win parliamentary approval.

Source: Canadian Senate Special Committee on Illegal Drugs, *Cannabis: Our Position for a Canadian Public Policy*. Ottawa: Senate of Canada, 2002, pp. 624–25.

One goal of the Netherlands' policy of tolerating marijuana use was to encourage users to stay inside mainstream society rather than join a "drug scene," populated by outcasts and criminals, where they would likely come in contact with harder drugs.

## Legalization would bring in more revenue.

The costs of marijuana prohibition are substantial. According to the Justice Policy Institute, America's drug-control budget grew from $65 million in 1969 to nearly $19.2 billion in 2003. The vast majority of that spending goes toward disrupting supply, catching sellers and users, and processing them through the criminal justice system. Decriminalizing marijuana would also save taxpayers money, although the savings would be more modest because the police would still be arresting users. Backers of a successful 2008 ballot proposal that decriminalized the drug in Massachusetts estimated that the new policy would save state taxpayers about $29.5 million a year in law-enforcement costs. That is consistent with what the Connecticut Law Revision Commission found: "Studies of states that have reduced penalties for possession of small amounts of marijuana have found that ... expenses for arrests and prosecution of marijuana possession offenses were significantly reduced."[4] In Australia, states that decriminalized marijuana discovered that the change brought in more revenue from fines and, at the same time, allowed authorities to spend less on enforcement.

If marijuana were legal, the government would be able to tax it. California's marijuana crop alone is valued at $18 billion, and most economic activity associated with that crop is currently untaxed. In 2005, Jeffrey Miron, a professor at Harvard University, estimated that legal marijuana would bring in $2.4 billion a year in revenue if it were taxed like other goods, and $6.2 billion a year if the government taxed it at rates comparable to those on alcohol and tobacco. Legalization might also create numerous spinoff industries that would hire workers and bring in revenue in the form of sales and income taxes. Already in California, the legalization of medical marijuana has led to the creation of businesses such as stores that sell high-tech growing equipment, marijuana "clubs" that pay rent and hire workers, marijuana-themed magazines and food products, and chains of for-profit clinics with doctors who specialize in recommending medical marijuana. Full legalization could create still more businesses—for example, in advertising, tourism, and sales of smoking paraphernalia and ingredients used to make edible marijuana products.

## Legalization would reduce violent crime.

The prohibition of alcohol in the United States coincided with a sharp increase in the murder rate during the 1920s and early 1930s. Many of these murders were committed by organized criminals fighting for control of the illegal liquor trade. Marijuana prohibition, too, has led to organized criminals fighting deadly "turf wars." Legalizing marijuana would greatly reduce the number of black-market suppliers as well as conflict among them and with the authorities. A panel of the New York City Bar argued: "Common sense indicates that without the immense profits guaranteed by the necessarily restricted nature of the outlets, there would be little advantage to maintaining such black markets. The current patterns of drug-sale related turf violence would be substantially, if not wholly, undermined."[5] For that reason, more than 500 economists, led by Nobel Prize winner Milton Friedman, sent President George W. Bush an open letter asking for "an open and honest debate" about marijuana prohibition—a debate that, in their view, would likely end up endorsing legalization.

In 1982, a National Academy of Sciences panel observed: "There has been violence in marijuana-growing regions in the United States. The extent of such violence is not known with any precision, but there have been popular press reports of kidnappings, assaults, burglaries, and homicides known to be connected with the marijuana business."[6] Since then, drug-related organized crime has become more widespread and more violent. The National Drug Intelligence Center's 2008 *National Drug Threat Assessment* reported:

The threat associated with marijuana trafficking and abuse is rising, largely the result of a growing demand for high-potency marijuana as well as a concomitant

## The Economics of Legalizing Marijuana

In 2005, Jeffrey Miron, a visiting professor of economics at Harvard University, wrote a paper titled *The Budgetary Implications of Marijuana Prohibition*. His work was sponsored by the Marijuana Policy Project, which opposes marijuana prohibition.

Miron cautioned that the budgetary impact would not, by itself, determine the wisdom of prohibition. Nevertheless, he said that the costs required to enforce marijuana prohibition, and the consequences of not taxing the drug, were relevant to a rational discussion of marijuana policy. Miron estimated that legalization would save state and local governments a total of about $5 billion per year. Those savings fell into three categories:

- **Law-enforcement costs.** Miron estimated that 50 percent of marijuana arrests were due solely to possession of the drug, and not on some independent offense such as weapons possession. Using that assumption, he calculated that police departments spent $1.71 billion on arrests for possession only.

- **Justice system costs.** Miron found that about 11 percent of felony convictions were the result of marijuana charges, which amounted to $2.94 billion spent to prosecute marijuana offenders.

- **Prison costs.** Miron estimated that one percent of prisoners were there on marijuana charges, resulting in an estimated cost of $484 million to keep them in prison.

Those three categories add up to $5.1 billion in savings, which would be offset by $100 million in lost revenue: If marijuana were legalized, the police could not seize assets from those caught with marijuana, and courts could not collect fines from convicted marijuana users.

In addition, the federal government spent $13.6 billion on interdiction—disrupting the supply—of all drugs. Miron multiplied that figure by the percentage of marijuana arrests and convictions as a percentage of all drug arrests and convictions, and came up with an estimate of $2.6 billion spent on marijuana interdiction alone. He adjusted that figure down to $2.39 million to account for lost forfeiture and fine revenue if the drug were legalized.

increase in the drug's availability. An increase in domestic cannabis cultivation by DTOs [drug trafficking organizations] contributes to this threat, particularly the

Next, Miron estimated the extra taxes the federal government and the states would collect under legalization. He started with the Office of National Drug Control Policy's estimate that Americans spent an estimated $10.5 billion a year on the drug. He assumed that legalization would not affect demand for marijuana, a conservative assumption because some people who would like to use the drug avoid it out of fear of getting arrested. (On the other hand, increased use of marijuana might come at the expense of alcohol and tobacco, which are legal and taxed; and some people might be less attracted to marijuana if it lost its "forbidden fruit" status.)

Miron assumed that if marijuana were legal, the cost to the supplier would likely remain the same. Suppliers in a legal market would not have to pay fines or have their assets seized, and would not risk being put out of business as the result of going to prison. They would, however, incur new costs, such as taxes. At the retail level, Miron estimated, based on the experience of countries with more liberal marijuana laws, that the price of marijuana would fall by 25 percent. Thus, under legalization, Americans would spend about $7.9 billion a year on marijuana.

Finally, Miron offered two different assumptions about how the government would tax marijuana. The first assumption was that the government would tax it at the same rate as other consumer goods. In that case, tax revenue would be in the neighborhood of $2.4 billion. (Miron asserted that most Americans would buy the drug from legal suppliers rather than grow their own, just as few Americans make their own alcohol.) The second assumption was that the government would treat marijuana the way it treats alcohol and tobacco and impose a "sin tax" on top of the taxes levied on consumer goods in general. Miron argues that the government could impose a high sin tax without creating a black market. He pointed to Europe, where cigarette taxes in many countries account for 75 percent to 85 percent of the price. A 50-percent "sin tax," on top of other taxes, would yield a total of $9.5 billion a year, minus some lost revenue because of black market activity and reduced consumption because of the higher price.

Source: Jeffrey A. Miron, *The Budgetary Implications of Marijuana Prohibition*. Washington, D.C.: Marijuana Policy Project, 2005, http://www.prohibitioncosts.org/mironreport. html.

recent expansion of cultivation operations by Mexican, Asian, and Cuban DTOs.[7]

In Latin America, drug cartels have become so powerful that they represent a security threat to a number of countries in that region. Recognizing that, a commission headed by the former presidents of Brazil, Colombia, and Mexico recommend that governments in the Western Hemisphere consider decriminalizing marijuana in order to reduce the violence and corruption associated with trafficking in illegal drugs.

## Education and treatment are more effective than prohibition.

Even if criminal penalties were abolished, society could still educate people, especially young people, about the dangers of using the drug. In fact, if marijuana were legal, the government would be free to use more effective approaches than the current ones that rely heavily on fear. A panel of the New York City Bar concluded: "Because of its penchant for exaggeration and cartoonish treatment of the issues, most current education about drugs is not taken seriously by young people. As a result, it is far less effective than other health education (e.g., about nutrition, fitness, and smoking cigarettes)."[8] The editors of *Consumer Reports* added that much anti-drug publicity is counterproductive because it actually makes the drugs more attractive. If marijuana were legalized, education efforts could be shifted from promoting abstinence to reducing the overall risks of marijuana use, especially heavy use. The Canadian Senate committee recommended: "Harm reduction strategies related to cannabis should include information on the risks associated with heavy chronic use, tools for detecting at-risk and heavy users and measures to discourage people from driving under the influence of marijuana."[9]

Ending marijuana prohibition would not stop businesses from keeping the drug—and intoxicated employees—out of the workplace. Applicants still could be required to pass a drug test before being offered a job. Employees who drove company vehicles or operated machinery could be tested for drug use, and those who tested positive could be subject to disciplinary action. In fact, employers would be free to ban any use of marijuana on the job, just as many workplaces ban smoking and forbid employees to drink alcohol during working hours.

Legal marijuana would remain off-limits for young people. In all probability, the minimum age for using the drug would be at least as high as it is for tobacco—either 18 or 19, depending on the state. Schools would have the power to ban the drug from school property, as they do with alcohol and tobacco. In addition, they would retain the power to discourage off-campus use. In *Board of Education of Independent School District No. 92 of Pottawatomie County v. Earls* (2002), the U.S. Supreme Court ruled that it was constitutional for schools to require students taking part in extracurricular activities to take drug tests, at least if the tests were random and those who tested positive were not reported to the police. School officials also have the authority to bring in drug-sniffing dogs and physically search students who are suspected of carrying substances banned by school rules. These tactics have been found constitutional.

Finally, treating people who have marijuana-related health problems is a better use of resources than catching and punishing users. California voters made that determination in 2000, when they approved Proposition 36, a law that offers tens of thousands of nonviolent drug offenders a chance to enter treatment rather than go to jail or prison. According to a study by the University of California, Los Angeles, every dollar spent on treatment under this law saves the state's taxpayers between $2.50 and $4. Legalization also would reduce the number of people in treatment who do not require it. According to the U.S. Department of Health and Human Services, more than half of those who went into treatment for marijuana did not meet the criteria for dependence set out in the *Diagnostic and Statistical Manual of Mental Disorders.*

## Tolerating marijuana has not caused serious problems elsewhere.

The Canadian Senate panel, which recommended legalizing the drug, downplayed concerns that relaxing marijuana laws would cause a significant increase in use. Based on the experience of other countries that had relaxed their laws, the panel predicted that legalizing the drug in Canada would produce a short-term increase in use, followed by a "roller-coaster" pattern of rising and falling usage rates. More recently, Peter Reuter, a professor at the University of Maryland, observed: "What would happen if the drug were legalized? The Dutch de facto legalization of sale through coffee shops is the closest available experience. The most striking observation is that marijuana use in that country is lower than in many other European countries and a lot lower than in the United States."[10]

The European Monitoring Centre for Drugs and Drug Addiction found that 22.6 percent of Dutch citizens between ages 15 and 64 reported having used cannabis in their lifetime. That compares with 30 percent of British citizens and 26.2 percent of French citizens in that age group, even though both countries have stricter marijuana laws. In the United States, which takes an even harder line toward the drug, 40 percent of adults have used it. The Canadian Senate committee observed:

> [C]ountries with a very restrictive approach, such as Sweden and the United States, are poles apart in terms of cannabis use levels and that countries with similar liberal approaches, such as the Netherlands and Portugal, are also at opposite ends of the spectrum . . . We have concluded that public policy itself has little effect on cannabis use trends and that other more complex and poorly understood factors play a greater role in explaining the variations.[11]

**Health Matters**

# Drug rankings differ

*An evidence-based system proposed by British researchers for ranking a drug's harmfulness rates marijuana as less harmful than many legal drugs.*

## What research says

Rates drugs on a scale of 0 to 3 for three factors in each of three categories; higher numbers equal more harmful rating

**Total**
(Out of possible 9 points)

| Factors | |
|---|---|
| Physical harm | • Acute, chronic, intravenous |
| Risk of dependency | • Pleasure, psychological dependence, physical dependence |
| Social costs | • Intoxication, social harm, health-care costs |

**Heroin**
| 2.78 | 3.0 | 2.54 | 8.32 |

**Cocaine**
| 2.33 | 3.0 | 2.17 | 6.89 |

**Alcohol**
| 1.4 | 1.93 | 2.21 | 5.54 |

**Tobacco**
| 1.24 | 2.21 | 1.42 | 4.87 |

**Marijuana**
| .99 | 1.51 | 1.5 | 4.0 |

## What laws say …

### … in the U.S.

Under the Controlled Substances Act of 1970, marijuana is classified as a Schedule I substance*

**Some of the drugs included in Schedule I (a felony)**

*High potential for abuse; no currently accepted medical use; lack of safety for use under medical supervision

• Heroin
• LSD
• Ecstasy
• **Marijuana**

### …and in the U.K.

Some claim the ABC system does not give specific information about a drug's risks

| Class A | • Heroin | • Cocaine |
| (most harmful) category | • LSD | • Ecstasy |
| | • Crystal meth | • Magic mushrooms |

| Class A/B | • Amphetamines |

| Class C | • **Marijuana** | • Ketamine |

Source: BBC, Medical News Today, Advisory Council on the Misuse of Drugs
Graphic: Lee Hulteng                    © 2010 MCT

This table shows recommendations by British researchers for reclassifying the harmfulness of drugs. The evidence-based system they employed shows marijuana to be less harmful than many legal drugs. In 2009, Britain upgraded marijuana to Class B.

In Australia, which once had tough marijuana laws, three states have experimented with decriminalization. According to the Canadian Senate committee, there were few serious side effects: "Cannabis use did increase in South Australia over the period from 1985 to 1995 but this was so throughout Australia, including in jurisdictions with a total prohibition approach to cannabis. In fact, the largest increase in the rate of weekly cannabis use . . . occurred in Tasmania, a prohibitionist state."[12] Much the same thing has happened in the United States. Eleven states have adopted some form of decriminalization. These states have not reported a spike in marijuana use. In fact, the Connecticut Law Revision Commission found that states that treated possession as a criminal offense experienced larger increases in usage than states that had decriminalized. In California, which has comparatively liberal marijuana laws, marijuana use is below the national average. One possible explanation is that Californians, even those who have never used the drug, are more knowledgeable about its effects. Another is that lower levels of enforcement have removed the drug's "forbidden fruit" appeal.

## Summary

Decades of marijuana prohibition have bred violence and corruption. Prohibition has resulted in the waste of billions of dollars on law-enforcement efforts, which have not stopped people from using the drug. Ending prohibition would dry up the black market and enable government to regulate the marijuana industry. Buyers could expect better and safer marijuana, and would rarely come into contact with criminals or hard drug users. A legal-marijuana industry could bring in billions of dollars in tax revenue and spur economic growth. Even if penalties for using the drug were eliminated, society would have a variety of tools to fight abuse, including school and workplace anti-drug policies and educational efforts. The experience of other countries, as well as some states in this country, suggests that relaxing marijuana laws would not lead to widespread abuse of the drug.

# The Future of Marijuana Policy

It has been more than a generation since marijuana emerged as a major social concern. For a while, it appeared that the United States would one day decriminalize the drug or even allow possession and use in private. Some states did eliminate criminal penalties for possessing or using small amounts of marijuana. In the 1980s, however, momentum swung back toward the traditional policy of prohibition. Most policymakers support tough laws aimed at achieving a drug-free America. Nevertheless, a growing number of Americans question the wisdom of marijuana prohibition and are looking for alternatives.

## Prohibition Versus Harm Reduction

Other Western countries have begun to move away from the American model of drug prohibition. As one substance-abuse specialist remarked to the Canadian Senate committee: "It is evident in U.S. drug policy that, the people for whom drug use is a moral issue, the cost is unimportant. The costs are irrelevant to them. What is relevant is making sure that the use of drugs is seen as wrong."[1] Officials in many countries are embracing an alternative policy known as *harm reduction,* which attempts to reduce the overall damage resulting from the use of drugs without insisting on abstinence. Backers of harm reduction insist theirs is a more realistic approach to the drug problem. The Canadian Senate committee found that such an approach was also consistent with human nature: "No matter how attractive calls for a drug-free society might be, and even if some people might want others to stop smoking, drinking alcohol, or smoking joints, we all realize that these activities are part of our social reality and the history of humankind."[2]

Harm reduction gained support during the 1980s when public officials found that addicts who injected drugs with shared needles had a higher rate of diseases such as AIDS and hepatitis. Instead of rigorously enforcing drug prohibition, those officials decided it would be more humane to provide addicts with needle-exchange programs and supervised places to inject. Harm-reduction principles were also behind the Netherlands' decision to tolerate the use of marijuana. Dutch officials believed that left to their own devices, young people would experiment with marijuana for a short time, then stop using it. That apparently happened: The Netherlands has a relatively low usage rate. The Dutch also believed that providing a semi-legal means of obtaining marijuana would reduce the chances that young users would use hard drugs.

Policymakers question drug prohibition for another reason. Studies indicated that strict drug laws had little impact on usage, were costly to enforce, and damaged some users' lives by leaving them with a criminal record. Worldwide, there has been an overall trend toward lessening the punishment for marijuana use. In Europe, a number of countries have decriminalized the drug. These countries adopted that policy by various means: The

Netherlands has a policy of official tolerance; the parliaments of Portugal and Russia decriminalized the possession of small amounts; and Germany's Constitutional Court handed down a ruling that discourages prosecutors from bringing criminal charges against small-time offenders. Elsewhere in the world, a number of Latin American countries and several Australian states have adopted some form of decriminalization.

Not all countries, however, have moved to liberalize their laws. In 2009, Britain upgraded marijuana from Class C, one of the least dangerous drugs, to Class B. Those caught with the drug are once again subject to arrest and criminal penalties. The year before, Swiss voters turned down a proposal under which marijuana would be legalized along the lines of alcohol. Even in the Netherlands, public officials are having second thoughts. Amsterdam officials adopted new regulations that will reduce the number of marijuana-selling coffeehouses.

## America's Marijuana Policy

In the United States, there is deep-seated resistance to the concept of harm reduction. Many Americans cannot accept a key assumption of harm reduction—namely, accommodating people's illegal recreational drug use. Our country has a long tradition of obeying the law, and our legislators have often passed laws intended to stop behavior most of us consider immoral. Another reason for not liberalizing the laws is our treaty commitments. The United States was instrumental in bringing about today's international drug-control system under which countries pledge to punish the nonmedical use of a variety of drugs, including marijuana. Supporters of our current policy argue that if America relaxes its marijuana laws, it would send the wrong message to the world. America is the world's number-one user of recreational drugs, and thus has an added responsibility to curb that use.

Furthermore, most public officials believe that the war on drugs is winnable, and that progress is being made. The Drug

The 1938 propaganda film *Tell Your Children* was later reissued under such titles as *Dope Addict, Doped Youth, Love Madness,* and most famously, *Reefer Madness.* In the film, two characters seduce local high school students into smoking marijuana, which leads to the total ruination of all concerned. Such films grew out of the policies of the Progressive Era of the early twentieth century.

Enforcement Administration argues forcefully in favor of continuing the fight against drugs: "Moreover, our fight against drug abuse and addiction is an ongoing struggle that should be treated like any other social problem. Would we give up on education or poverty simply because we haven't eliminated all problems?"[3]

This is not to say that all Americans favor marijuana prohibition. In July 2009, a CBS News survey found that 41 percent of Americans favored making marijuana legal. An October 2002 *Time*/CNN poll found 72 percent support for doing away with jail time as a punishment for marijuana possession, and opinion surveys have consistently shown that a large majority of Americans support medical marijuana. In fact, a consensus appears to be developing that using marijuana is wrong, but the laws punish it too severely. Even though proposals to legalize marijuana outright have lost at the polls, there is support for more modest efforts to liberalize the laws. In 2008, Massachusetts voters approved a proposal that downgraded marijuana possession to a civil offense, punishable by a maximum $100 fine.

## Federal Power Versus States' Rights

In the United States, the debate over marijuana policy is complicated by our system of government. Since 1914, the federal government has regulated drugs under its power to tax and later on, its power to regulate interstate commerce. David Musto, a professor at the Yale School of Medicine, observed that the Harrison Act typified the mentality of the Progressive Era of the early twentieth century. Progressives saw problems such as drug addiction as national in scope, and proposed uniform federal laws, as opposed to a patchwork of state laws, to address them. In addition, all 50 states regulate marijuana as part of their police powers. As the U.S. Supreme Court observed: "States traditionally have had great latitude under their police powers to legislate as to the protection of the lives, limbs, health, comfort, and quiet of all persons."[4] Many state laws are modeled after the federal Controlled Substances Act.

*(continues on page 116)*

# Marijuana Policy in Other Countries

### Other English-speaking countries

In 2009, Great Britain upgraded marijuana from Class C, the least harmful category of illegal drugs, to Class B. Simple possession of marijuana is once again an offense subject to arrest after six years during which an offender was given a "police caution" that resulted in no criminal penalties but could be brought up if he or she went to court on some other charge. Critics argue that the government upgraded marijuana for political reasons, noting that a scientific panel had recommended keeping the drug in Class C.

In Australia, marijuana laws vary by state. Some states have passed laws under which a person charged with possessing a small amount of marijuana can avoid going to court by paying a modest, on-the-spot fine. Even in states that still treat possession as a crime, first offenders are commonly put on probation or sent to counseling.

Canada still classifies marijuana possession as a crime, but most offenders are fined, put on probation, or ordered to perform community service. In 2003 and 2004, the Liberal Party introduced legislation that would make possession of less than 15 grams punishable by a fine only, but that legislation failed to pass. As of mid-2010, the government favors tougher, not more liberal, drug laws.

### Europe

Since 1976, the Netherlands has had a policy of de facto decriminalization. Laws against marijuana are still on the books, but Dutch authorities follow a policy of not prosecuting possession or use of small amounts. Authorities also tolerate the sale and use of small amounts in coffee shops in communities that allow them. Coffee shops must follow certain rules, including not selling alcohol or allowing teenagers on the premises. Amsterdam has closed a number of coffee shops because they were too close to schools, and two Dutch border towns outlawed the shops because they attract "pot tourists."

In recent years, a number of other countries have decriminalized the possession of small amounts of marijuana, either by an act of parliament, a court ruling, or official policy. Those countries include Belgium, Germany, Italy, Portugal, Russia, and Spain. Offenders are still subject to administrative sanctions, typically a fine, although some offenders could lose their driver's license or right to carry a gun. In 2008, voters in Switzerland rejected a proposal that would have legalized and regulated marijuana along the lines of alcohol.

At the other end of the spectrum is Sweden, which is considered to have Western Europe's toughest marijuana laws. During the late 1960s, that country moved toward a zero-tolerance policy, as well as the goal of a "drug-free Sweden." Possession of marijuana is punishable by a jail term, but first offenders are generally fined. The government sponsors an intensive anti-drug campaign that teaches Swedes that "drug careers" start with marijuana. The zero-tolerance policy enjoys overwhelming public support. The laws of France also take a hard line, treating possession of any amount of marijuana a crime punishable by up to a year in jail. In several other countries, the law spells out jail terms for possession, but offenders are typically fined or given a warning by the police.

## Latin America

Most countries in the region have followed the American approach of prohibition, enforced by tough criminal penalties. In recent years, however, some countries have liberalized their laws. In 1994, Colombia decriminalized the possession of 20 grams (0.7 ounces) or less. Argentina, Brazil, and Venezuela also have eliminated jail as punishment for possession of personal-use quantities of the drug. Mexico, which is experiencing serious problems with drug-related crime, decriminalized the possession of small amounts of marijuana, as well as heroin and cocaine, in August 2009. Also in 2009, the Latin American Commission on Drugs and Democracy, headed by three former presidents from that region, recommended that Latin American countries consider decriminalizing marijuana.

## Asia

In general, drug laws are much stricter in Asia than they are in the West. In Singapore, traffickers can face long prison terms and possibly the death penalty. Even the possession of small amounts can lead to a jail sentence, and the police can test suspected users for drugs. Malaysia is equally strict with traffickers; and according to the U.S. State Department, a person found with 200 grams (7 ounces) of marijuana is presumed by law to be a trafficker. Japan, South Korea, and Taiwan all treat the possession of even small amounts of marijuana as a criminal offense, and the maximum penalty for possession is higher than it in this country.

## The Middle East

Countries in the Middle East generally take a hard line against drugs. In Saudi Arabia, a person found with illegal drugs—a category that even extends to alcohol—can be sentenced to public flogging as well as imprisonment. The penalty for drug trafficking is death. In the United Arab Emirates, possession of even trace amounts of marijuana can result in a four-year prison sentence.

*(continued from page 113)*

Until 1996, when California voters legalized medical mari-juana in that state, differences between federal and state mari-juana laws were not a serious problem. The passage of medical marijuana laws, however, has touched off a legal battle between federal authorities and medical-marijuana providers. The federal government, like the Progressives, argues that drug laws should be uniform across the country. For that reason, the administra-tions of presidents Bill Clinton and George W. Bush waged a vigorous legal battle against medical-marijuana providers in California and other states. The federal government won an important victory when the Supreme Court ruled in *Gonzalez v. Raich* (2005) that the CSA authorized the federal government to deny patients access to medical marijuana, even if state law made it legal. In *Raich,* however, the Court did not rule that the CSA made state medical-marijuana laws inoperative.

Although state authorities will not make arrests for medical marijuana in states where it is legal, federal authorities reserve the right to do so. That said, there are signs that the Obama admin-istration will be more sympathetic to states' rights; the Justice Department indicated that it would stop raiding clinics in states where medical marijuana is legal. Raids, however, might resume in the future. To stop that from happening, Representative Barney Frank of Massachusetts introduced the Medical Marijuana Patient Protection Act,[5] which would move marijuana from Schedule I of the CSA to Schedule II and bar the federal government from prosecuting dispensaries, doctors, patients, and caregivers act-ing in compliance with state medical-marijuana laws. Frank's approach might someday succeed. In 2007, a federal appeals court observed, "For now, federal law is blind to the wisdom of a future day when the right to use medical marijuana to alleviate excruciat-ing pain may be deemed fundamental. Although that day has not yet dawned, considering that during the last ten years eleven states have legalized the use of medical marijuana, that day may be upon us sooner than expected."[6]

With respect to recreational marijuana use, support for prohibition is not uniform across the country. In fact, attitudes differ within many states. Some cities, such as Seattle and Denver, have declared the enforcement of marijuana laws "the lowest law-enforcement priority," a symbolic gesture but an indication of local anti-prohibition sentiment. Some observers believe that it is only a matter of time before states begin to repeal, or at least relax, laws banning the possession and use of marijuana. Even though the CSA would still prohibit marijuana in those states, federal authorities lack the resources to pursue small-time offenders. For that reason, they concentrate on major traffickers in the drug.

In *Gonzales v. Raich*, the Supreme Court found that "we have no difficulty concluding that Congress had a rational basis for believing that failure to regulate the intrastate manufacture and possession of marijuana would leave a gaping hole in the CSA."[7] Supporters of uniform national legislation argue that if some states legalize marijuana, they will undercut other states' efforts to curb its use. Some point out that the legalization of gambling in some states forced legislators elsewhere to do the same or else lose tax revenue. Others believe that jurisdictions with liberal laws will attract dealers and hard-core users. Still others worry about "pot tourism." When the Netherlands decriminalized marijuana, it attracted visitors from neighboring countries, many of whom continued to use the drug when they returned home.

On the other hand, some advocates believe that it is healthy for states to experiment with new policies. The Sentencing Project favors repeal of federal marijuana laws, leaving marijuana policy up to state and local governments. Supporters of this approach agree with Supreme Court Justice Louis Brandeis that "a single courageous state may, if its citizens choose, serve as a laboratory; and try novel social and economic experiments without risk to the rest of the Country."[8]

If states move to legalize marijuana, the federal government has several options. One is to arrest and prosecute providers of legal marijuana, as they have done with medical marijuana. Another is to use the spending power to pressure states to keep marijuana illegal. In 1984, Congress passed legislation that required states to raise their drinking age to 21 or else lose part of their federal highway funds. In *South Dakota v. Dole* (1987), the Supreme Court upheld the law as constitutional, reasoning that Congress had the power to impose conditions on the money it appropriates. Finally, it could amend the CSA. Representative Barney Frank introduced the Personal Use of Marijuana by Responsible Adults Act of 2009.[9] His legislation would do away with federal penalties for the possession of marijuana, or the transfer of marijuana between adults, for personal use.

## What Is Decriminalization?

In recent years, some advocates have contended that the nation's policy of making marijuana use a crime does not curb the use of the drug and has resulted in substantial economic and social costs. They have urged public officials to consider alternatives.

One approach, which has been recommended by several panels of experts, is *legalization*. Making the drug legal does not necessarily mean creating a completely free market, like that for coffee or soft drinks. Most supporters of legalization propose a heavily regulated market. For example, legislation that would legalize marijuana in California is modeled after the state's alcoholic-beverage-control system.

An intermediate approach, taken in some jurisdictions here and in some other countries, is *decriminalization*—that is, taking a behavior or activity outside the scope of the criminal justice system. There are several methods of decriminalizing behavior. One is to eliminate all penalties for engaging in it. In 1972, the Shafer Commission proposed doing so for marijuana use in private. That is the law in only one state—Alaska—and that is the result of a court decision, not an act of the legislature.

Another form of decriminalization is downgrading possession—and, in many cases, the not-for-profit transfer—of marijuana from a criminal offense to a civil

## Finding Common Ground

Since 1914, the official policy of the United States has been the elimination of recreational drug use. During the 1960s and early 1970s, marijuana policy shifted from elimination to what the Shafer Commission called "containment"—trying to prevent the drug from spreading any farther. Beginning in the 1980s, a drug-free America once again became a national objective, even though the Shafer Commission had warned: "The primary goals of a prudent marijuana social control policy include preventing irresponsible use of the drug, attending to the consequences of such use, and deemphasizing use in general. Yet an absolute prohibition of possession and use inhibits the ability of other

offense. During the late twentieth century, most states reclassified minor traffic violations, such as speeding, as noncriminal offenses and began referring to them as "civil infractions" or "violations." People charged with such offenses are not taken into custody or fingerprinted; the penalty is a relatively small fine, on the order of $100, with no possibility of jail time; and the violator does not have a criminal record.

Several states have downgraded marijuana possession to civil-offense status; federal law allows a U.S. attorney to treat the possession of a small quantity as a civil offense, though the maximum fine is $10,000. A number of other states, such as New York, treat possession of small amounts as a low-level misdemeanor that is not punishable by jail and which the criminal justice system treats more like a civil offense than a crime.

There is also a distinction between *de jure* decriminalization, which involves a change in the law as written, and *de facto* decriminalization, where the criminal law remains on the books but the authorities have made an official decision not to prosecute violators. De jure decriminalization has occurred in a few countries in Europe and Latin America. The best-known example of de facto decriminalization is the Netherlands, which in 1976 adopted an official policy of tolerance toward possession and use of small amounts of marijuana, as well as the sale of small amounts—with a number of restrictions—in coffeehouses.

institutions to contribute actively to these objectives."[10] Some argue that drug use can never be reduced to zero and propose instead that the government try to limit the number of drug users to an "irreducible minimum."

Many experts argue that we pay too much attention to whether a drug is legal and not enough to the dangers associated with using it—people often assume that legal drugs are safe and illegal drugs are dangerous. The editors of *Consumer Reports* point out that any drug can be harmful if abused and urge that we put drug use in perspective:

> Society, laws, and law-enforcement policies already differentiate the occasional drinker of a glass of wine or

## Legalized Marijuana in California?

In March 2009, Tom Ammiano, a state legislator from San Francisco, introduced Assembly Bill 390, "The Marijuana Control, Regulation, and Education Act." Ammiano and other supporters of the legislation argued that legalization would generate much-needed tax revenue; legalize an industry that already accounts for California's number-one cash crop; protect the environment by ending clandestine, and often destructive, cultivation of marijuana on public land; and free up police and justice system resources to concentrate on more serious offenses.

The legislation would license and regulate commercial cultivators, wholesalers, and retailers of marijuana. The state could charge up to $5,000 for an initial license and $2,500 a year to renew it. Licensees would have to pass a background check, and not hire people younger than 21. Cultivators would be required to provide adequate security to protect against unauthorized access to the marijuana crop, inspect and track marijuana, and comply with record-keeping requirements. Wholesalers would have to follow state regulations governing the sale and packaging of marijuana. Retailers would be forced to keep marijuana behind a counter in an area not directly accessible to customers, store it in a case that is locked between sales, and not sell it to anyone younger than 21. Penalties for underage beer, the social drinker, the problem drinker, the spree drinker, the chronic drunk, and the alcoholic. Similar distinctions should be made with respect to various modes of use of marijuana.... It is one thing to get stoned on marijuana on Saturday night; it is quite another to stay stoned all day every day.[11]

Ultimately, whether marijuana should be legal and how violators should be treated are questions that must be answered by lawmakers who, in turn, must answer to voters. Since marijuana first appeared, America's policy toward it has been heavily influenced by public opinion. Sometimes the public has been manipulated, and sometimes passion has triumphed over logic. Even if

sales of marijuana would be equivalent to those for underage sales of alcohol. Marijuana sold at retail would be taxed at $50 an ounce.

Current laws that impose criminal and civil penalties for cultivation, possession, or sale of marijuana would be repealed. The legislation would allow people 21 and older to use marijuana in private. Public use would be an infraction, punishable by a fine. It would be legal to transport marijuana in a vehicle, but illegal to use it inside a vehicle. Selling or giving marijuana to a person younger than 21 would be an infraction punishable by a fine of up to $100. Likewise, underage possession or use would be an infraction.

A person 21 or older would be allowed to cultivate up to 10 mature cannabis plants, provided that the plants were not visible from a public place. Unlawful cultivation would be an infraction.

The legislation would also remove marijuana from the state's controlled-substances law; repeal drug-paraphernalia laws to the extent that they apply to items used to smoke marijuana; and end civil forfeiture of items, such as cars or boats, connected with the sale or use of marijuana.

Assembly Bill 390 failed to get out of committee. Supporters of legalization, however, collected enough petition signatures to put a similar proposal on the November 2010 ballot.

emotions again run high in the debate over marijuana, however, the Shafer Commission offers these words of reassurance: "[I]t is unlikely that marijuana will affect the future strength, stability or vitality of our social and political institutions. The fundamental principles and values upon which the society rests are far too enduring to go up in the smoke of a marijuana cigarette."[12]

## Summary

In the United States, marijuana prohibition remains the law of the land. Some advocates favor a policy of harm reduction, which accepts drug use as inevitable and seeks to make that use safer without requiring abstinence. That approach, however, is contrary to America's tradition of respect for the law, and some believe it would set a bad example for other countries. Medical marijuana caused a conflict between the federal government, which strictly prohibits it, and those states that have legalized it. A similar conflict is likely if states attempt to legalize the drug. Although support for legalization has grown, most Americans still oppose it. Recreational marijuana use will likely remain illegal in the foreseeable future, and debate over the drug is likely to continue for years to come.

## Beginning Legal Research

The goals of each book in the POINT/COUNTERPOINT series are not only to give the reader a basic introduction to a controversial issue affecting society, but also to encourage the reader to explore the issue more fully. This Appendix is meant to serve as a guide to the reader in researching the current state of the law as well as exploring some of the public policy arguments as to why existing laws should be changed or new laws are needed.

Although some sources of law can be found primarily in law libraries, legal research has become much faster and more accessible with the advent of the Internet. This Appendix discusses some of the best starting points for free access to laws and court decisions, but surfing the Web will uncover endless additional sources of information. Before you can research the law, however, you must have a basic understanding of the American legal system.

The most important source of law in the United States is the Constitution. Originally enacted in 1787, the Constitution outlines the structure of our federal government, as well as setting limits on the types of laws that the federal government and state governments can enact. Through the centuries, a number of amendments have added to or changed the Constitution, most notably the first 10 amendments, which collectively are known as the "Bill of Rights" and which guarantee important civil liberties.

Reading the plain text of the Constitution provides little information. For example, the Constitution prohibits "unreasonable searches and seizures" by the police. To understand concepts in the Constitution, it is necessary to look to the decisions of the U.S. Supreme Court, which has the ultimate authority in interpreting the meaning of the Constitution. For example, the U.S. Supreme Court's 2001 decision in *Kyllo v. United States* held that scanning the outside of a person's house using a heat sensor to determine whether the person is growing marijuana is an unreasonable search—if it is done without first getting a search warrant from a judge. Each state also has its own constitution and a supreme court that is the ultimate authority on its meaning.

Also important are the written laws, or "statutes," passed by the U.S. Congress and the individual state legislatures. As with constitutional provisions, the U.S. Supreme Court and the state supreme courts are the ultimate authorities in interpreting the meaning of federal and state laws, respectively. However, the U.S. Supreme Court might find that a state law violates the U.S. Constitution, and a state supreme court might find that a state law violates either the state or U.S. Constitution.

Not every controversy reaches either the U.S. Supreme Court or the state supreme courts, however. Therefore, the decisions of other courts are also important. Trial courts hear evidence from both sides and make a decision, while appeals courts review the decisions made by trial courts. Sometimes rulings from appeals courts are appealed further to the U.S. Supreme Court or the state supreme courts.

Lawyers and courts refer to statutes and court decisions through a formal system of citations. Use of these citations reveals which court made the decision or which legislature passed the statute, and allows one to quickly locate the statute or court case online or in a law library. For example, the Supreme Court case *Brown v. Board of Education* has the legal citation 347 U.S. 483 (1954). At a law library, this 1954 decision can be found on page 483 of volume 347 of the U.S. Reports, which are the official collection of the Supreme Court's decisions. On the following page, you will find samples of all the major kinds of legal citation.

Finding sources of legal information on the Internet is relatively simple thanks to "portal" sites such as findlaw.com and lexisone.com, which allow the user to access a variety of constitutions, statutes, court opinions, law review articles, news articles, and other useful sources of information. For example, findlaw.com offers access to all Supreme Court decisions since 1893. Other useful sources of information include gpo.gov, which contains a complete copy of the U.S. Code, and thomas.loc.gov, which offers access to bills pending before Congress, as well as recently passed laws. Of course, the Internet changes every second of every day, so it is best to do some independent searching.

Of course, many people still do their research at law libraries, some of which are open to the public. For example, some state governments and universities offer the public access to their law collections. Law librarians can be of great assistance, as even experienced attorneys need help with legal research from time to time.

# Common Citation Forms

| Source of Law | Sample Citation | Notes |
|---|---|---|
| **U.S. Supreme Court** | *Employment Division v. Smith*, 485 U.S. 660 (1988) | The U.S. Reports is the official record of Supreme Court decisions. There is also an unofficial Supreme Court ("S. Ct.") reporter. |
| **U.S. Court of Appeals** | *United States v. Lambert*, 695 F.2d 536 (11th Cir.1983) | Appellate cases appear in the Federal Reporter, designated by "F." The 11th Circuit has jurisdiction in Alabama, Florida, and Georgia. |
| **U.S. District Court** | *Carillon Importers, Ltd. v. Frank Pesce Group, Inc.,* 913 F.Supp. 1559 (S.D.Fla.1996) | Federal trial-level decisions are reported in the Federal Supplement ("F. Supp."). Some states have multiple federal districts; this case originated in the Southern District of Florida. |
| **U.S. Code** | Thomas Jefferson Commemoration Commission Act, 36 U.S.C., §149 (2002) | Sometimes the popular names of legislation—names with which the public may be familiar—are included with the U.S. Code citation. |
| **State Supreme Court** | *Sterling v. Cupp*, 290 Ore. 611, 614, 625 P.2d 123, 126 (1981) | The Oregon Supreme Court decision is reported in both the state's reporter and the Pacific regional reporter. |
| **State Statute** | Pennsylvania Abortion Control Act of 1982, 18 Pa. Cons. Stat. 3203-3220 (1990) | States use many different citation formats for their statutes. |

## Cases

### *People v. Sinclair*, 387 Mich. 91, 194 N.W.2d 878 (1972)

The Supreme Court of Michigan unanimously overturned the conviction of radical figure John Sinclair, who was sentenced to 10 years in prison for giving two marijuana cigarettes to undercover police officers. Even though the justices agreed on the result, they offered a variety of reasons for doing so.

### *State v. Ravin*, 537 P. 2d 494 (Alaska 1975)

The Supreme Court of Alaska ruled that the right to privacy under that state's constitution extended to adults who use marijuana in their homes. After marijuana use by young Alaskans rose during the late 1970s, citizen groups tried to overturn this decision. Legal experts, however, believe that *Ravin* remains the law in that state.

### *In the Matter of Marijuana Rescheduling Petition*, Drug Enforcement Administration Docket No. 86-22 (September 6, 1988)

Activists have filed a number of petitions with the Drug Enforcement Administration seeking to have marijuana moved from Schedule I of the CSA to a less-restrictive schedule, which might enable doctors to prescribe it. One petition resulted in a hearing before an administrative law judge, who recommended that marijuana be placed in Schedule II because it had an accepted medical use in *In the Matter of Marijuana Rescheduling Petition*. The DEA, however, rejected his recommendation. In 2001, the DEA rejected another such petition. In its Notice of Denial of Petition, *Federal Register* 66, no. 75 (April 18, 2001), the agency concluded that marijuana had a high potential for abuse and thus belonged in Schedule I. Both DEA decisions refusing to reclassify marijuana were later upheld by federal appeals courts.

### *United States v. Oakland Cannabis Buyers' Cooperative*, 532 U.S. 483 (2001)

The U.S. Supreme Court rejected a marijuana dispensary's defense of "medical necessity," which would have shielded it from prosecution under the CSA for selling marijuana to patients who qualified for it under California law.

### *Conant v. Walters*, 309 F.3d 629 (9th Cir. 2002)

A federal appeals court ruled that the government violated doctors' right to free speech when it threatened to strip doctors of the ability to prescribe federally controlled drugs if they recommended marijuana to their patients.

### *Board of Education of Independent School District No. 92 of Pottawatomie County v. Earls*, 536 U.S. 822 (2002)

The U.S. Supreme Court ruled that it was constitutional for public school districts to drug-test students who participated in extracurricular activities. Courts in a few states have reached the opposite result because of broader privacy protection in state constitutions. One such decision is *York v. Wahkiakum School District*, 163 Wash.2d 297, 178 P.3d 995 (Sup. Ct. 2008).

### *Gonzalez v. Raich,* 545 U.S. 1 (2005)

In a lawsuit brought by Angel Raich, the U.S. Supreme Court ruled that the CSA applies to the use of medical marijuana, even if the drug never crosses state lines and the amount involved is small. The Court sent the case back to the lower courts to dispose of Raich's other arguments. In *Raich v. Gonzales,* 500 F.3d 850 (9th Cir. 2007), a federal appeals decided not to address her claim of medical necessity because she had not been prosecuted for marijuana possession.

## Statutes

### Marijuana Tax Act (50 Stat. 551, Public Law 75-238)

The first federal law dealing with marijuana, it was strictly speaking a tax measure, but its effect was to make the drug all but illegal in this country.

### Controlled Substances Act

The Controlled Substances Act is Title II of Comprehensive Drug Abuse Prevention and Control Act of 1970 (Public Law 91-513), and is codified as 21 U.S.C. §§801 and following. The CSA's most important feature is a classification system under which drugs are assigned to "schedules" with varying levels of regulation. Marijuana was placed in Schedule I, meaning that it has a high potential for abuse and no recognized medical use. The CSA also sets out federal penalties for possessing or trafficking in illegal drugs. Marijuana and other drugs are also regulated at the state level, typically by laws modeled after the CSA. In many states, the penalties for possessing or using small amounts of marijuana are less severe than under federal law. More than a dozen states explicitly rule out jail as a punishment for first offenders caught with small amounts.

### Proposition 215

In 1996, California voters approved Proposition 215 (codified as *California Health & Safety Code* §11362.5), which allows qualified patients to possess and use marijuana on a doctor's recommendation. As of 2010, 14 states have enacted some form of medical-marijuana law. These laws do not override the federal CSA, and both doctors and patients can still be prosecuted under federal law.

## Terms and Concepts

1-delta-9-trans tetrahydrocannabinol (THC)
Addiction/dependency
Black market
"Broken windows" policy
Cannabis
Cash crop
Civil violation
Commerce Clause

Compassionate Use Act
Controlled Substances Act (CSA)
Decriminalization
De facto/de jure
Deterrence
Drug Enforcement Administration (DEA)
Excise taxes
Federalism
Freedom of speech
"Gateway drug"
Harm reduction
Harrison Narcotic Act
Harry Anslinger
"Marijuana tourism"
Medical necessity
Plea bargaining
Police powers
"Polydrug" use
Potency
Privacy
Prohibition
Public service announcements
"Quality of life" offenses
*Reefer Madness*
Search and seizure
Rehabilitation
Selective enforcement
Shafer Commission
"Sin" taxes
Single Convention on Narcotic Drugs
Social costs
"Victimless crime"
"War on drugs"
work ethic
"Zero tolerance" policing

## Introduction: Marijuana and Prohibition

1 Assembly Bill 390, 2009–10 California Legislature.

2 National Institute on Drug Abuse, *Marijuana Abuse: Research Report.* October 2002, p. 3, http://www.drugabuse.gov/PDF/RRMarijuana.pdf.

3 Edward M. Brecher, et al., *Licit and Illicit Drugs.* Boston: Little, Brown, 1972, p. 409.

4 National Commission on Marijuana and Drug Abuse, *Marijuana: A Signal of Misunderstanding: The Report of the National Commission on Marijuana and Drug Abuse.* Washington, D.C.: U.S. Government Printing Office, 1972, p. 10.

5 38 Stat. 785.

6 Brecher, et al., *Licit and Illicit Drugs,* p. 49.

7 50 Stat. 551, Public Law 75-238.

8 National Commission on Marijuana and Drug Abuse, *Marijuana,* p. 105.

9 *Ibid.*

10 Public Law 91-513.

11 National Commission on Marijuana and Drug Abuse, *Marijuana,* p. 105.

12 *California Health & Safety Code* §11362.5(b)(1)(A).

13 *United States v. Oakland Cannabis Buyers' Cooperative,* 532 U.S. 483, 491 (2001).

## Point: Government Should Protect People from Marijuana

1 National Commission on Marijuana and Drug Abuse, *Marijuana: A Signal of Misunderstanding: The Report of the National Commission on Marijuana and Drug Abuse.* Washington, D.C.: U.S. Government Printing Office, 1972, p. 24.

2 Office of National Drug Control Policy, *Marijuana Myths & Facts: The Truth Behind 10 Popular Misperceptions.* Washington, D.C., undated, p.7.

3 National Institute on Drug Abuse, *Marijuana Abuse: Research Report.* Rockville, MD, 2005, p. 2, http://www.drugabuse.gov/PDF/RRMarijuana.pdf.

4 John Walters, "The Myth of 'Harmless' Marijuana," *Washington Post,* May 1, 2002.

5 National Commission on Marijuana and Drug Abuse, *Marijuana,* p. 45.

6 Office of National Drug Control Policy. *Marijuana Myths & Facts,* p. 9.

7 World Health Organization, *Cannabis: A Health Perspective and Research Agenda.* Geneva, Switzerland, 1997, p. ii.

8 Office of National Drug Control Policy. *Marijuana Myths & Facts,* p. 2.

9 U.S. Department of Transportation news release, "Recent Analysis Shows that One in Six High School Seniors Admitted Driving While High," September 16, 2003.

10 Canadian Senate Special Committee on Illegal Drugs, *Cannabis: Our Position for a Canadian Public Policy.* Ottawa: Senate of Canada, 2002, p. 18.

11 Notice of Denial of Petition, *Federal Register* 66, no.75, p. 20047 (April 18, 2001).

12 Congressional Research Service, *Medical Marijuana: Review and Analysis of Federal and State Policies.* Washington, D.C., 2008, p. 46.

13 "Western States Back Medical Marijuana," MSNBC.com, November 4, 2004, http://www.msnbc.msn.com/id/6406453/.

## Counterpoint: Marijuana Does Not Cause Serious Harm

1 National Academy of Sciences, *An Analysis of Marijuana Policy.* Washington, D.C.: National Academies Press, 1982, p. 4.

2 Daniel Forbes, "The Myth of Potent Pot," Slate.com, November 19, 2002, http://www.slate.com/id/2074151.

3 Marsha Rosenbaum, *Safety First: A Reality-Based Approach to Teens and Drugs.* New York: Drug Policy Alliance Network, 2007, p. 9, http://www.safety1st.org/images/stories/pdf/safetyfirst.pdf.

4 *In the Matter of Marijuana Rescheduling Petition,* Drug Enforcement Administration Docket No. 86-22 (September 6, 1988).

5 National Commission on Marijuana and Drug Abuse, *Marijuana: A Signal of Misunderstanding. The Report of the National Commission on Marijuana and Drug Abuse.* Washington, D.C.: U.S.

Government Printing Office, 1972, p. 90.

6 Canadian Senate Special Committee on Illegal Drugs, *Cannabis: Our Position for a Canadian Public Policy*. Ottawa: Senate of Canada, 2002, p. 151.

7 *Ibid.*, p. 2.

8 *Ibid.*, p. 27.

9 Janet E. Joy, Stanley J. Watson Jr., and John A. Benson Jr., *Marijuana and Medicine: Assessing the Science Base*. Washington, D.C., National Academies Press, 1999, p. 6.

10 National Commission on Marijuana and Drug Abuse, *Marijuana*, p. 439.

11 Jeremy Laurance, "Tobacco and Alcohol 'Are More Dangerous than LSD,'" *Independent* (U.K.), March 23, 2007.

12 Edward M. Brecher, et al., *Licit and Illicit Drugs*. Boston: Little, Brown, 1972, p. 205.

## Point: Marijuana Should Remain Illegal

1 National Commission on Marijuana and Drug Abuse. *Marijuana: A Signal of Misunderstanding. The Report of the National Commission on Marijuana and Drug Abuse*. Washington, D.C.: U.S. Government Printing Office, 1972, p. 27.

2 *Ibid.*, pp. 8–9.

3 *Ibid.*, p. 133.

4 Edward M. Brecher, et al., *Licit and Illicit Drugs*. Boston: Little, Brown, 1972, p. 522.

5 National Commission on Marijuana and Drug Abuse, *Marijuana*, p. 132.

6 Latin American Commission on Drugs and Democracy, *Drugs & Democracy: Toward a Paradigm Shift*. Monterrey, Mexico, 2009, p. 26.

7 *Ibid.*, p. 27.

8 Office of National Drug Control Policy, *Marijuana Myths & Facts: The Truth Behind 10 Popular Misperceptions*. Washington, D.C., undated, p. 15.

9 Canadian Senate Special Committee on Illegal Drugs, *Cannabis: Our Position for a Canadian Public Policy*. Ottawa: Senate of Canada, 2002, p. 398.

10 Office of National Drug Control Policy, *Who's Really in Prison for Marijuana*. Washington, D.C., 2005, p. 9.

11 *Ibid.*, p. 27.

12 Drug Enforcement Administration, *Speaking Out Against Drug Legalization*. Washington, D.C., 2003, p. 12, http://www.dea.gov/demand/speakout/index.html.

13 *Ibid.*, p. 5.

14 National Institute on Drug Abuse, *Marijuana Abuse: Research Report*. Rockville, Md., 2005, http://www.drugabuse.gov/PDF/RRMarijuana.pdf

15 Office of National Drug Control Policy, *Marijuana Myths & Facts*, p. 22.

## Counterpoint: Enforcing Marijuana Prohibition Is Destructive and Wasteful

1 Eric Schlosser, "Reefer Madness," *Atlantic Monthly*, August 1994.

2 Peter Brady, "From Utah to Abu Ghraib," *Cannabis Culture*, November 1, 2004, http://www.cannabisculture.com/v2/articles/3581.html.

3 Connecticut Law Revision Commission, *Drug Policy in Connecticut and Strategy Options*. Hartford, Conn., 1997, http://www.cga.ct.gov/lrc/DrugPolicy/DrugPolicyRpt2.htm.

4 Justice Policy Institute, *Efficacy and Impact: The Criminal Justice Response to Marijuana Policy in the United States. Executive Summary*, Washington, D.C., 2005, http://www.csdp.org/research/efficacyexecsum.pdf, p. 3.

5 Schlosser, "Marijuana and the Law," *Atlantic Monthly*, November 1994.

6 National Commission on Marijuana and Drug Abuse, *Marijuana: A Signal of Misunderstanding. The Report of the National Commission on Marijuana and Drug Abuse*, Washington, D.C., 1972, p. 160.

7 Edward M. Brecher, et al., *Licit and Illicit Drugs*, Boston: Little, Brown, 1972, p. 60.

8 Jon Gettman, et al., *United States Marijuana Arrests, Part Two: Racial Differences in Drug Arrests*. Washington, D.C.: National Organization for the Reform

of Marijuana Laws, 2000, http://www.norml.org/index.cfm?Group_ID=5326.

9 Ryan S. King, *Disparity By Geography: The War on Drugs in America's Cities.* Washington, D.C.: The Sentencing Project, 2008, p. 9, http://sentencingproject.org/Admin%5CDocuments%5Cpublications%5Cdp_drugarrestreport.pdf.

10 Canadian Senate Special Committee on Illegal Drugs, *Cannabis: Our Position for a Canadian Public Policy.* Ottawa: Senate of Canada. 2002, p. 126.

11 Brecher, et al. *Licit and Illicit Drugs*, p. 539.

12 *Ibid.*, p. 433.

## Point: Relaxing Marijuana Laws Would Cause Serious Problems

1 Association of the Bar of the City of New York, *A Wiser Course: Ending Drug Prohibition.* New York, 1994, http://www.druglibrary.org/schaffer/library/studies/nylawyer/nylawyer.htm.

2 John Walters, "Our Drug Policy Is a Success." *Wall Street Journal*, December 5, 2008.

3 National Commission on Marijuana and Drug Abuse, *Marijuana: A Signal of Misunderstanding. The Report of the National Commission on Marijuana and Drug Abuse.* Washington, D.C.: U.S. Government Printing Office, 1972, p. 82.

4 Drug Enforcement Administration, *Speaking Out Against Drug Legalization.* Washington, D.C., 2003, p. 6, http://www.dea.gov/demand/speakout/index.html.

5 National Commission on Marijuana and Drug Abuse, *Marijuana*, p. 149.

6 "If Marijuana Is Legal, Will Addiction Rise?," Room for Debate blog, July 19, 2009, http://roomfordebate.blogs.nytimes.com/2009/07/19/if-marijuana-is-legal-will-addiction-rise.

7 National Commission on Marijuana and Drug Abuse, *Marijuana*, p. 149.

8 Canadian Senate Special Committee on Illegal Drugs, *Cannabis: Our Position for a Canadian Public Policy. Summary Report.* Ottawa, 2002, p. 34.

9 Asa Hutchinson, Opening Statement, Yale University Law School Debate with New Mexico Governor Gary Johnson, "The Past, Present, & Future of the War on Drugs," November 15, 2001, New Haven, Conn., http://www.usdoj.gov/dea/speeches/s111501.html.

10 Marcus Wohlsen and Lisa Leff, "California Sprouts Marijuana 'Green Rush.'" MSNBC.com, July 18, 2009, http://www.msnbc.msn.com/id/31981559/ns/us_news-life/.

11 National Commission on Marijuana and Drug Abuse, *Marijuana*, p. 147.

## Counterpoint: Regulating Marijuana Is Wiser Than Prohibiting It

1 Edward M. Brecher, et al., *Licit and Illicit Drugs.* Boston: Little, Brown, 1972, p. 417.

2 *Ibid.*, p. 265.

3 *Ibid.*, p. 265.

4 Connecticut Law Revision Commission, *Drug Policy in Connecticut and Strategy Options.* Hartford, Conn., 1997, http://www.cga.ct.gov/lrc/DrugPolicy/DrugPolicyRpt2.htm.

5 Association of the Bar of the City of New York, *A Wiser Course: Ending Drug Prohibition.* New York, 1994. http://www.druglibrary.org/schaffer/library/studies/nylawyer/nylawyer.htm.

6 National Research Council, *An Analysis of Marijuana Policy.* Washington, D.C.: National Academies Press, 1982, p. 16.

7 National Drug Intelligence Center, *National Drug Threat Assessment 2008.* Washington, D.C.: U.S. Department of Justice, 2007, p. 13, http://www.usdoj.gov/ndic/pubs25/25921.

8 Association of the Bar of the City of New York, *A Wiser Course.*

9 Canadian Senate Special Committee on Illegal Drugs, *Cannabis: Our Position for a Canadian Public Policy. Summary Report.* Ottawa, 2002, p. 28.

10 "If Marijuana Is Legal, Will Addiction Rise?," Room for Debate blog, July 19, 2009, http://roomfordebate.blogs.nytimes.com/2009/07/19/if-marijuana-is-legal-will-addiction-rise.

11 Canadian Senate Special Committee on Illegal Drugs, *Cannabis*, p. 45.

12 *Ibid.*, p. 555.

## Conclusion: The Future of Marijuana Policy

1 Canadian Senate Special Committee on Illegal Drugs, *Cannabis: Our Position for a Canadian Public Policy. Summary Report*. Ottawa, 2002, p 380.

2 *Ibid.*, p. 38.

3 Drug Enforcement Administration, *Speaking Out Against Drug Legalization*. Washington, D.C., 2003, p. 2.

4 *Medtronic Inc. v. Lohr*, 518 U.S. 470, 475 (1996).

5 H.R. 2835, 111th Congress.

6 *Raich v. Gonzales*, 500 F.3d 850, 866 (9th Cir. 2007).

7 *Gonzales v. Raich*, 545 U.S. 1, 22 (2005).

8 *New State Ice Company v. Liebmann*, 285 U.S. 262, 311 (1932) (Brandeis, J., dissenting).

9 H.R. 2943, 111th Congress.

10 National Commission on Marijuana and Drug Abuse, *Marijuana: A Signal of Misunderstanding. The Report of the National Commission on Marijuana and Drug Abuse*. Washington D.C.: U.S. Government Printing Office, 1972, p. 143.

11 Edward M. Brecher, et al., *Licit and Illicit Drugs*. Boston: Little, Brown, 1972, p. 526.

12 National Commission on Marijuana and Drug Abuse, *Marijuana*, p. 102.

## Books and Reports

Association of the Bar of the City of New York. *A Wiser Course: Ending Drug Prohibition.* New York, 1994. Available online. URL: http://www. druglibrary.org/schaffer/library/studies/nylawyer/nylawyer.htm.

Brecher, Edward M., et al. *Licit and Illicit Drugs.* Boston: Little, Brown, 1972.

Canadian Senate Special Committee on Illegal Drugs. *Cannabis: Our Position for a Canadian Public Policy.* Ottawa: Senate of Canada, 2002.

Connecticut Law Revision Commission. *Drug Policy in Connecticut and Strategy Options.* Hartford, Conn., 1997. Available online. URL: http:// www.cga.ct.gov/lrc/DrugPolicy/DrugPolicyRpt2.htm.

Drug Enforcement Administration. *Speaking Out Against Drug Legalization.* Washington, D.C., 2003. Available online. URL: http://www.dea.gov/ demand/speakout/index.html.

Gettman, Jon, et al. *United States Marijuana Arrests, Part Two: Racial Differences in Drug Arrests.* Washington, D.C.: National Organization for the Reform of Marijuana Laws, 2002. Available online. URL: http://www. norml.org/index.cfm?Group_ID=5326.

King, Ryan S. *Disparity By Geography: The War on Drugs in America's Cities.* Washington, D.C.: The Sentencing Project, 2008.

King Ryan S., and Marc Mauer. *The War on Marijuana: The Transformation of the War on Drugs in the 1990s.* Washington, D.C.: The Sentencing Project, 2005. Available online. URL: http://www.sentencingproject.org/ Admin%5CDocuments%5Cpublications%5Cdp_waronmarijuana.pdf.

Miron, Jeffrey A. *The Budgetary Implications of Marijuana Prohibition.* Washington, D.C.: Marijuana Policy Project, 2005. Available online. URL: http://www.prohibitioncosts.org/mironreport.html.

National Academy of Sciences. *An Analysis of Marijuana Policy.* Washington, D.C.: National Academies Press, 1982.

National Commission on Marijuana and Drug Abuse. *Marijuana: A Signal of Misunderstanding. The Report of the National Commission on Marijuana and Drug Abuse.* Washington, D.C.: U.S. Government Printing Office, 1972.

National Drug Information Center. *National Drug Threat Assessment 2009.* Washington, D.C.: U.S. Department of Justice, 2008. Available online. URL: http://www.usdoj.gov/ndic/pubs31/31379/31379p.pdf.

Office of National Drug Control Policy. *Who's Really in Prison for Marijuana?* Washington, D.C., 2005.

———. *The President's National Drug Control Strategy, 2008 Annual Report.* Washington, D.C., 2009.

## Articles

Schlosser, Eric. "Marijuana and the Law," *Atlantic Monthly*, October 1994.

———. "Reefer Madness," *Atlantic Monthly*, September 1994.

## Web Sites

### The American Civil Liberties Union
*http://www.aclu.org*
> The nation's oldest and best-known civil-liberties organization is primarily concerned with police practices that may violate the Bill of Rights.

### The Drug Policy Alliance Network
*http://www.drugpolicy.org*
> This group focuses on all drugs, not just marijuana. It opposes prohibition and has been instrumental in getting medical marijuana laws passed.

### The Libertarian Party
*http://www.lp.org*
> This is a political party that favors minimal government intrusion and on that basis opposes laws against recreational drug use.

### National Institute on Drug Abuse
*http://www.nida.nih.gov*
> A number of other federal agencies, such as the National Institute on Drug Abuse, are responsible for studying the effects of drug use and the nation's drug policy. State and local authorities are responsible for enforcing state drug laws, and most arrests for marijuana offenses are made at this level.

### The National Organization for the Reform of Marijuana Laws
*http://www.norml.org*
> Established in 1970, this organization favors decriminalization of the drug as a first step toward legalization. NORML also supports medical-marijuana laws.

### The Office of National Drug Control Policy

*http://www.whitehousedrugpolicy.gov*

This office, which is part of the Executive Office of the President, sets drug-control goals and develops strategies for attaining them. This agency is headed by the nation's "drug czar," who has little actual power but is very influential in the debate over drug policy.

### The Partnership for a Drug-Free America

*http://www.drugfree.org*

This is a nonprofit organization that aims to educate Americans, parents in particular, about the dangers of using drugs.

### The U.S. Justice Department

*http://www.justice.gov*

This government agency is generally responsible for enforcing federal criminal laws. Within the Justice Department, the Drug Enforcement Administration (http://www.dea.gov) is responsible for enforcing the Controlled Substances Act, and is also in charge of classifying controlled drugs.

# PICTURE CREDITS ||||▷

**PAUL RUSCHMANN, J.D.,** is a legal analyst and author based in Canton, Michigan. He received his undergraduate degree from the University of Notre Dame and his law degree from the University of Michigan. He is a member of the State Bar of Michigan. His areas of specialization include legislation, public safety, traffic and transportation, and trade regulation. He is the author of numerous books in the POINT/COUNTERPOINT series, dealing with such issues as the military draft, indecency in the media, private property rights, the war on terror, and global warming. He can be found online at www.paulruschmann.com.

**ALAN MARZILLI, M.A., J.D.,** lives in Birmingham, Ala., and is a program associate with Advocates for Human Potential, Inc., a research and consulting firm based in Sudbury, Mass., and Albany, N.Y. He primarily works on developing training and educational materials for agencies of the federal government on topics such as housing, mental health policy, employment, and transportation. He has spoken on mental health issues in 30 states, the District of Columbia, and Puerto Rico; his work has included training mental health administrators, nonprofit management and staff, and people with mental illnesses and their families on a wide variety of topics, including effective advocacy, community-based mental health services, and housing. He has written several handbooks and training curricula that are used nationally and as far away as the territory of Guam. He managed statewide and national mental health advocacy programs and worked for several public interest lobbying organizations while studying law at Georgetown University. He has written more than a dozen books, including numerous titles in the POINT/COUNTERPOINT series.